Esther: Queen at the Crossroads

Esther: Queen at the Crossroads

by

JEANETTE LOCKERBIE

MOODY PRESS

CHICAGO

Printed in the United States of America

Contents

1
Setting the Stage of History

We suggest that you choose another queen more worthy than she (1:19, TLB).

Read Esther 1:1-22

Can the most ordinary event be turned into the opportunity of a lifetime? Think of something that has happened to you. Perhaps you attended a certain function with no more expectation than of passing a pleasant hour or two. But before the evening was over, something or someone new entered your life. At the time, this may not have seemed life changing, but later you were able to pinpoint the very time—the exact word or phrase—the precise location where your life was channeled into a different course.

In like manner the history of nations is shaped and reshaped.

The book of Esther is the drama of a nation. More, it is the deliverance of a nation: significant reading in a day when evil forces appear to be in unchallenged control of God's universe, for history is the revelation of providence.

Not once does the name of God appear in these ten chapters, nor does the word "providence"; yet God and His providential intervention permeate every chapter and event in the book of Esther.

As always, both drama and deliverance involve characters major and minor. Little did they think that they were cast for a prominent role in the history of the Jewish people. The year is 482 B.C. The Medo-Persian emperor Ahasuerus (Xerxes of secular history) is about to invade Greece in what eventuated in the battle of Thermopylae and Salamis.

Who could know that what started out as a lavish feast designed to impress the high military on the eve of a strategic battle, would in fact be scene one: the stage setting for an historic chain of immortalized events?

The book opens on this festive note, a scene that for sheer luxury and splendor would by contrast make our social event of the season look like a hastily prepared potluck supper. The color scheme is outlined for us, and right royal it is! Not only red carpet—here was carpet of red, white, and blue on a floor of alabaster and marble. For reclining, there were couches of gold and of silver, and the golden drinking cups were strictly one of a kind.

If your curiosity is further aroused—and what woman does not want to know everything that is to be known about a party—you may read a modern counterpart of Ahasuerus' feast. *Time* Magazine, October 25, 1971, covers the extravaganza hosted by the Shah of Iran (ancient Persia), at a cost of $100,000. The guest list included nine kings, five queens, thirteen princes, eight princesses, and sixteen presidents. The occasion marked the 2500 year anniversary of the founding of the Persian Empire by Cyrus the Great.

Nothing is said of the food at King Ahasuerus' feast—just that he served "royal wine in abundance."

THE QUEEN HAS HER OWN PARTY

It is significant to note that God uses women as well as men to further His plans.

Queen Vashti comes into the picture. We are not told much about her. From the little we do know, we can assume she was of a haughty disposition. She was beautiful: no mistaking that.

Her name—in the old Persian language—means beautiful woman.[1] In this, Vashti was akin to Sarah and Sarah's daughter-in-law, Rebekah.

There is nothing wrong with being beautiful, though in some Christian circles people seem to feel that God is not the author of beauty! Delete the fact of a beautiful woman and the part she plays in the drama that is the book of Esther—and it is watered down until there is no plot.

Shushan, the palace, had never been more festive, both the king and the queen separately entertaining their guests.

Banquets in those days were not 8 P.M. to midnight affairs. The revelry hit a slump, and the king's party began to pall on the seventh day, and it was then he had an idea. He would send for his queen, his beautiful queen, and show her off. What better treat could he offer his guests than a feast for their eyes?

To do proper honor to the royal Vashti, the king sent seven VIPs from his court to escort her to the feast. But far from proudly leading their queen into the presence of her husband the king, the seven chamberlains returned to report her refusal to attend his banquet.

Some have speculated that Vashti had every right to resolutely deny the king's request that she appear. One school of thought has it that she was observing the culture of the day. No woman, says this school, would in that day and culture permit any man except her own husband to see her. If he had not been drinking heavily, he would have respected this custom and would not have required her to appear before all the men at his feast.

This line of thought is, of course, refuted when Esther, who would not be less modest nor less mindful of the culture, invited Haman, not once but twice, to her banquet.

Vashti might have refused out of consideration for her own guests.

Whatever Vashti's reason for disobeying her husband's

1. *International Standard Bible Encyclopedia,* 5:3046.

wishes, we do not know. We do know that she was a key
character in an intriguing plan, as was Rahab that day she
opened her door to the Hebrew spies and gained a place in
history; as was Ruth, when forsaking her pagan deities she
chose to follow her mother-in-law, thereby gaining a place in
the lineage of Christ; as women in every generation have been,
for evil or for good. Who can dispute, for instance, that Susan-
nah Wesley was a history-shaper, although her sons, John and
Charles, are credited with the revival that affected England
spiritually, socially, and morally in their day. And what of
the unheralded Sunday school teacher who makes her indelible
imprint on a boy or girl, who, won to Christ through this
teacher, then goes on to be a history-shaper for God?

Back to Vashti. We can imagine something of the repercus-
sions when the courtiers appeared without her. The palace
court was thronged with notables. Undoubtedly, the king had
announced the imminent arrival of his queen. He had been
envisioning her in all her beauty, garbed in royal apparel. What
a sight for all to enjoy and for him to glory in! His queen,
upon whose head he had chosen to place the royal crown.
And now—this!

THE RAMIFICATIONS OF VASHTI'S ACTION

Humiliation and cold fury raged in the heart of the wine-
sodden Ahasuerus. How dared Vashti so treat him—the king—
in the presence of personages he had spared no effort to impress? What would they think of all the grandeur he had displayed? All the bounty they had partaken of? In his mind
the king could hear their taunts: "A great monarch!" He fancied their scornful laughter would roll and echo throughout
the entire 127 provinces of his empire: laughter at his expense.
"A mighty warrior king—but he can't govern his own wife.
She mocks him—makes light of his commands."

Such brooding thoughts darkened the monarch's face, made
demons run rampant in his mind.

For us, in our emancipated civilization, it may be difficult for the significance of Vashti's refusal to strike home. "So she didn't choose to leave her own party at the king's bidding. What of it?" some may think. But things were far different in those days, as indeed they still are in many Eastern cultures. Not only was the king put down by a subject, but by a *woman*, even if she did happen to be the queen of the realm. A woman had no right to make such a choice. A woman was an inferior being, a chattel.

We might digress to say that of all the benefits and by-products of Christianity, none stands out more than the changes rung in the status of womanhood. In a special sense, Jesus Christ is woman's best friend. In some areas of the world the prevailing philosophy is that a woman has no soul. It follows, then, that the men have no concern about a future life for their women. In fact, a good cow or a goat is more prized than a woman in some countries.

Because of our own privileged position in a Christ-oriented society, it may be hard for some women to comprehend the problems of women in less favored circumstances. And some might have difficulty in comprehending that Vashti's blatant disobedience was such a colossal insult to the king.

THE PRICE OF DISOBEDIENCE

It appears that infuriated though he was, the king could not determine by himself just what punishment would fit Vashti's crime. He called in his wise men to advise him. Now whatever else characterized the Medes and Persians, they appeared to have had a hearty regard for their own laws. The queen had to be punished, no doubt about that. "But keep within what the law allows," the wise men agreed. ·

Before a verdict could be arrived at in the case of King Ahasuerus versus Queen Vashti, the evidence had to be reviewed and weighed.

"Not only has Queen Vashti wronged the king by her action," the lawyers considered, "she has likewise wronged all the princes and all the people in all the provinces of the King Ahasuerus." Far-reaching consequences!

Who could tell, they speculated, where the bad influence would end?

"Every woman in the empire will hear of it."

"Not one man will be safe from scorn."

"The women will despise every one of us unless this thing is nipped in the bud."

So went the discussion of the unprecedented flouting of a man's whim by his wife. "Contempt and wrath" would result unless stern measures were taken at once (v. 18). For if the queen, to whom all the women in the realm looked as their example, got away with such insubordination, what chance would any man have of being the head of his own house?

Failure to squelch such conduct as Vashti's could mean anarchy among the women.

However selfish and unspiritual the motive of these men who sat in judgment of the offending queen, their thinking coincides with God's Word in both Old and New Testament concerning the wife's subjection to her husband.

We need to keep in mind, of course, that this is a pagan situation, that here is a husband and wife neither of whom is in any degree governed by biblical principles, but by their own culture. However, since "All scripture is given by inspiration of God, and is profitable . . . for instruction in righteousness" (2 Timothy 3:16), there is a lesson for us even in the Vashti/Ahasuerus story. For despite all the modern outcries to the contrary, God's Word had never changed in its constancy that the husband is the God-ordained head of the home. As Ray Stedman has written, "You can't get around it, wives, no matter what version you use."[2]

It is not our purpose at this time to go into a discussion of the right and wrong of any husband's wishes. But we must go on record as stating that God does not issue directives which

2. Ray Steadman, *What Every Wife Should Know* (Rosemead, Calif.: Narramore, 1967).

a Christian wife finds impossible to obey. And with uncluttered simplicity the Bible says, "Wives, submit yourselves unto
your own husbands, as unto the Lord" (Ephesians 5:22).

How much heartache would be averted in modern society if
this and other related scriptural injunctions were heeded. (The
same principle applies to God's instructions to husbands.)

God created the first woman to be a helpmeet for her husband, and, at the fall, the Lord decreed, "Thy desire shall be
to thy husband, and he shall rule over thee" (Genesis 3:16).

The consequences of the wife's heeding or disregarding
God's command will have a strong bearing on the attitudes of
her children; her influence along this line will be far-reaching
in their lives—for good or bad.

Vashti's crime and its long-range effect having been summed
up by the wise men, it was now time for the sentence to be
pronounced. But the final word must come from the king
himself: "Depose Vashti and give her crown to someone
more worthy," was the recommended punishment.

"And the saying pleased the king" (v. 21).

How did Ahasuerus implement his decree? Did he debase
Vashti as publicly as she had humiliated him? Was the crown
literally torn from her brow? We can only speculate. What
we do know is that there was a scramble to call the translators
and scribes, for the word must needs be sent to all the provinces
and written so that every man could read and understand its
import.

The pronouncement "Every man should bear rule in his own
house" was as irrevocable as all the laws of the Medes and
Persians "that altereth not."

It *is* as irrevocable as the Word of God that liveth and
abideth forever.

Queen Vashti learned this truth the hard way. She came
and went on the stage of history renowned for only one act—
disobedience to her husband—and it cost her a throne. Yet,
in the providence of God she had a pivotal place in furthering
God's plan for His own people.

GOD HAS A PLAN

Everything in nature confirms that God has a master plan.

The four seasons unfailingly proclaim the fulfillment of God's revealed design (see Genesis 8:22).

The stars in their courses attest to God's controlling blueprinted plan. So predictable are the heavenly bodies that from our millions of miles away scientists can plot the course of a space vehicle and can rely on their findings and feel sure that no star will just "happen" to be in a particular place on a given day or hour or minute.

Because the tides of the sea are dependable to the precise minute, navigation can be totally determined by their ebb and flow.

The examples are endless.

It is extremely reassuring to us to keep such things in mind. We are living in days of unprecedented confusion among nations. Trust is almost nonexistent; disillusionment is fast replacing any vestige of credibility. More than ever we need a rock on which to stand. We need to realize that while men fumble and flounder, God knows what He is doing. As the wise Corrie Ten Boom has stated, "God has no *problems* with His world, just *plans* for it."[3]

Our encouragement comes from the certainty that God is sovereign, and He is working out His eternal blueprint. Nowhere is this illustrated more graphically and with such high drama as in the book of Esther.

To implement His plans, God uses *people*. A very few (e.g., Moses, Samuel, Esther, Mary, Joseph, John the Baptist, Paul) are aware of their role. Many are totally unaware, including Vashti, Ahasuerus, and Haman.

TO THINK ABOUT AND DO

1. Think back to some seemingly incidental happening that has had significant impact on your life.

3. Corrie Ten Boom, from message given at the Christian Booksellers Association, Dallas, 1973.

2. What kind of feelings does it give you to realize that the sovereign God of the universe is in charge of our planet earth? What fears does this knowledge allay?

3. If you had been in Vashti's place, what would you have chosen to do, and why?

4. What apparently justifiable reasons (according to vv. 10-11) would the queen have had for refusing the king's request?

5. After carefully reading and meditating on Ephesians 5:21-33, analyze and write down your personal reaction to these verses. Discuss how their teaching contrasts with the husband/wife relationship pictured in the book of Esther.

6. Queen Vashti forfeited a throne. In a Christian setting, what can it cost today's woman when she does not submit to her husband as the Scriptures make clear?

7. Just as Vashti, every one of us is remembered for something. For what kind of things do you *not* wish to be remembered? Ask yourself, What am I doing today to guard against being remembered only for negative things I have done or said?

8. What, in your opinion, is the most significant matter in this first chapter of the book of Esther?

2

The Cinderella of Shushan

Well, the king loved Esther more than any of the other girls. He was so delighted with her that he set the royal crown on her head (2:17, TLB).

Read Esther 2:1-19

"After these things."

After what things? A disgruntled king. A dethroned queen. A decree that brings delight to the men in the empire.

To each of us from time to time comes a plateau where we pause and reflect "after these things." Whether the musing brings joy or regret hinges entirely on our actions and interactions with other people during the course of the events.

Queen Vashti has exited from Shushan with her own unwritten thoughts. She is heard of no more, as far as the record is concerned.

THE BEAUTY CONTEST OF ALL TIME

King Ahasuerus is still with us, his bruised feelings salved. But he is minus a queen. Not for long is he left to ponder on Vashti's disobedience and dismissal, however. The court planners have gotten their heads together and plotted their scheme to replace her. A beauty contest, no less!

For someone other than the monarch of the Medes and Persians a marriage-maker would have sufficed. The dowry would have been agreed upon by the groom and the parents of the bride, and that would have been it. But for the king, all the most beautiful girls in the 127 provinces of his empire would parade, and he would make his choice.

Neither Atlantic City nor Miami Beach ever hosted such a contest. No Miss America or Miss Universe ever had such a prize dangled before her. No "Queen for a day, a dozen long-stemmed red roses, and a year of travel!" The winner of the Shushan pageant would wear the royal crown—with all that this meant in a proud empire.

The idea appealed to His Majesty, and he set the wheels in motion.

How could he, a royal despot commanding the lives of multitudes, know that, far from being in sole control of his own and others' fate, he himself was being manipulated on the stage of history?

God's ripening plot calls for additional characters.

On to the scene comes "a certain Jew" (2:5). God always has His certain man, His certain woman. He had His *Moses*— and a Gentile princess to fit into His plan for the special upbringing of the man who was already ordained to be the emancipator of his people. God had His *Joseph*—and a Gentile king (pharaoh) to elevate him to the position where he, too, was God's man to deliver his people from famine. God had His *Weizmann*. Like Mordecai, this man was concerned over the fate of his Jewish people. And God had His Winston Churchill to recognize Weizmann's contribution to his times. In 1949 Chaim Weizmann became the first president of the new nation of Israel.

Some would claim that God had His Moshé Dayan, Israel's defense minister. (Of the Six Day War, the mini-war in 1967, Dayan is reputed to have said, "This was our finest hour—or did it take that long?")

So, God had His *Mordecai* in the right place at the right time. Here was a Jew who could trace his ancestry back to the first family of Israel: he was a Benjamite (2:5). Neither captivity nor exile from his homeland could change the fierce loyalty and sense of destiny that being a Jew gave to Mordecai.

His position in the palace is not specified but it is clear that he lived within its confines. In the manner of a palace household in any era, in any country, news of coming events soon filtered to every member of the staff. Long before the announcement of the search for a beautiful queen to replace Vashti had gotten beyond the city gate, the palace of Shushan would be buzzing.

We can imagine some of the comments.

"Pretty girls—hundreds of them—from all over the empire."

"Will they ever find one as lovely as Vashti?"

"What will she look like?"

"How will she treat the other women in the king's harem?"

These and dozens of other questions, rumors, and speculations would keep tongues wagging, for, as the insightful Shakespeare wrote, "What the great do, the lesser prattle about."

THE NAME CONTESTANT

Mordecai kept his own counsel—but could a certain gleam in his eyes have been detected by a close observer? A gleam that spelled resolve—hope—and, yes, *faith?*

"Esther was brought also unto the king's house" (2:8).

Where, in all the kingdom—or in ten kingdoms—could any girl compare to his beautiful foster daughter, Hadassah (her Jewish name). Did his thoughts hark back to the day when, bereft of both parents, she had come to fill his home with her spritely gladness?

There was not a single doubt in Mordecai's mind. All it would take would be for the king to see her. Who could resist such charm and loveliness?

What of Esther herself? Did she shrink from this strange new thing that was happening to her? Did fears fill her heart at the prospect of being plucked from her own environment and planted in the king's palace with so many beautiful girls? Or was she secretly elated?

As Mordecai talked with her, no doubt assuring her that

he would be nearby and always anxious over what was happening to her, did she catch something of the dream that was his? And did this take the beauty contest out of the realm of personal possibilities into the area of patriotic challenge: challenge as to what she might be able to do, as queen, on behalf of her own people? Unquestionably, Mordecai must have had some precognition. Otherwise, would he have permitted his foster daughter to be put in the position of all the other girls? Jews do not countenance mixed marriages. A man of strong principles, Mordecai would have challenged the king's right to take Esther.

We can but speculate as to her feelings. Esther would not necessarily have studied the Old Testament Scriptures as most Jewish boys are required to do. She would not have learned the verses of comfort, consolation, and encouragement that are ours when we need special guidance and help (see Psalms 32:8; 73:24; Hebrews 13:5). She had no knowledge of the gracious promises Jesus would give us (e.g., John 15:5; 16:13) concerning the Holy Spirit's presence with us as believers.

Can you imagine your own thoughts in such a Cinderella situation?

If you are thinking, *I'm glad I live in a culture where I have a choice, where my feelings are considered in the important matter of marriage, where no arrangement can be made for me by a head of state, or by my parents or relatives,* then spare a compassionate prayer for the millions of young girls who do not have such freedom of choice.

Of course, in this instance there was the head-spinning part. And in the days that followed, Esther would have been less than the beautiful girl she was if dreams had not lit up her dark, luminous eyes.

All the loveliest young women in the empire were there—tall girls, short girls, rich girls, fair girls, dark girls, doubtless some like herself from the homes of the captives. Their fate for the next months was in the hands of the keeper of the women. Was Esther lonely? Did she long to be back with her own people?

Nearly a year spent among this group of glamorous girls could not but convince Esther that only by a miracle would she ever stand a chance of being chosen for the high position of queen. But daily, Mordecai walked in front of the court of the women to see how she did. Seeing him, was a conviction gradually borne in on her that a day of destiny was approaching, something she could neither explain to herself nor rationalize out of her mind?

"You, my child. You will take Vashti's place." In essence, had Mordecai impressed this upon her so that waking and sleeping she fancied she heard him pronounce his unshakeable belief?

APPOINTMENT WITH DESTINY

Then came the day of days. No longer was she a captive Cinderella. She was Esther, perfumed and gowned for her chance of a lifetime. Long before this day, she had won the favor of Hegai, into whose care all the beauties had been committed. If preferred treatment would help her win, this man was prepared to do his part in selecting her as queen.

But in the midst of the favorable circumstances, one discordant note sounds out. In obedience to Mordecai, as she had obeyed him since she was a child (2:20), Esther has not revealed her Jewish identity. For a whole year she had lived according to Gentile customs, eating only nonkosher food, not observing the religious holidays that are such a vital part of the practicing Jew.

One by one the lovely contestants had been rejected by the monarch. Not all the sweet perfumes of Arabia, nor all the arts of the robing mistress could turn out one beauty who pleased the fastidious Ahasuerus—until Esther, the pride of the "contest steward" (who undoubtedly helped to inspire confidence in her chances), was led into the presence of the king.

Did the heart of Ahasuerus do a double take when he saw her in all her unspoiled, fresh, young beauty, possibly so different, almost naive by contrast with the sophisticated misses who had preceded her?

We do not know. Very simply, in the way in which the Bible writers so often emphasize by seeming understatement, the record reads, "And the king loved Esther . . . and he set the royal crown on her head and made her queen" (2:18).

The new queen's reign began as the deposed Vashti's had ended, with a banquet. Esther was the guest of honor, and the occasion was marked by charitable and generous gestures on the part of King Ahasuerus. Things boded well for the young Jewess. But the day would come when being queen of the Medo-Persian Empire would spell other than popularity and pleasure for Esther.

For the present, it was a Cinderella story and all of our Christmases wrapped up into one, with all the pretty clothes, the partying, and the bounty.

The plans of "the certain Jew" had not miscarried. His confidence in his Hadassah had not been misplaced. With prophetic insight did he hug to himself the thought, "a Jewess in high places!" The foster daughter of an exile, her people captive—and now on her brow rested the royal crown!

Mordecai might have been pardoned for some justifiable glorying in the fact that "The mills of God grind slowly, but they grind."

We will leave Mordecai exactly where we first met him, at the palace gate. We have not heard the last of him, for although God is not once named in this significant Old Testament book, the Almighty has His hand on this certain Jew, for the survival of his nation. A background character seemingly playing a bit part, he will have his day in the limelight.

When twelve o'clock strikes, Esther is still in the royal palace, first lady in the realm, not a pawn of fate but a vital piece of God's long-range program. Esther—woman of destiny.

To Think About and Do

1. From the plan to replace Vashti through bringing in many girls for selection, what can we judge as to the culture of the Medo-Persians? In what ways does their contest differ with beauty contests as we know them? What are some of the ways in which a Miss America or a Tournament of Roses queen can be—and has been—honoring to Christ?

2. Which is more important to you, being in a place of service that is "normal" (acceptable to other Christians without question) or being in a place where you are sure God placed you, even though it may be difficult to explain to other Christians, and may be contrary to your own life-style?

3. What might have been some of the ways that Esther pleased Hegai (vv. 8-9)? Think about how your good attitudes—thoughtfulness, kindness, helpfulness—can be used to further your witness for Christ.

4. Write out some memorable incident in your own life when God unmistakably led you. What happened to yourself; to other people because of it?

5. Esther undoubtedly had many misgivings, even though she was not acting on her own volition and could not do anything about the situation. In contrast with Esther, what resources do we have when we especially need reassurance and guidance?

6. Mordecai must have had sound reasons for cautioning Esther against revealing her racial origin while she was in the palace for a year. What are your thoughts as to Mordecai's special guidance in those days? Very obviously, he was chosen for this strategic moment in history. In your opinion, does God specially endow those to whom He gives important assignments, or is it that God uses those whom He can depend upon to utilize what powers He has given them?

7. What, in your life, would qualify you for special service? Evaluate yourself and list these qualities, then ask God to use you this very week.

3

The High Cost of Being Different

*Now all the officials bowed before him [Haman] . . .
But Mordecai refused to bow* (3:2, TLB).

Read Esther 2:20–3:15

The wedding is over. Life in Shushan, the palace, is returning to normal after all the banqueting.

Quietly in the background, Mordecai is glorying in seeing his Esther elevated to the ranks of royalty: a Jewess among the Gentiles.

COINCIDENCE?

In the course of his own palace duties, one day Mordecai overhears a treacherous plot to assassinate King Ahasuerus, a happening not unknown in our own day of turmoil and bloody coups. The two would-be perpetrators apparently had reason to be angry. No doubt they would have carried out their scheme to murder the king. And again Mordecai moves into the situation. Surely he was God's man, in the right place at the right time, for who can tell what would have happened had Esther's husband been killed then.

Mordecai revealed the murderous plot to Esther. She told it to the king, in the name of Mordecai. "In his name." Three little words. But what a profound impact they were to have at a later date!

Investigation proved the story to be true. The would-be assassins were apprehended and hanged. Not only so, but in the presence of the king, the entire incident was recorded in the permanent court annals. Later we will see the significance of this record, for ultimately the fate of every Jew in the empire hinges on it.

Ahasuerus should have learned his lesson, but apparently he did not; history tells us that in the year 465 B.C. another pair succeeded in an identical plot.

What if Mordecai had not been where he was at the crucial time—or if he had held his peace, unwilling to become involved in Persian intrigue!

ENTER HAMAN

We move into chapter 3 of the book of Esther, and again we read, "After these things." The things referred to this time are the choosing of Esther the queen, and the foiling of the plot to kill King Ahasuerus.

The affairs of state are again occupying the glad-to-be-alive king. As always in high places, we can generally expect that there will be an apple-polisher; a social climber. In this instance he is Haman, a name as infamous in Jewish history as is his more modern counterpart, Hitler.

Who is Haman? What is his background? Some Bible scholars trace his ancestry to Agag, the king of the Amalekites (1 Samuel 15:8-33). Others, relying on their interpretation of the Samuel account as utter annihilation of the family of Agag, see "Haman, the Agagite" as locating his geographical background.[1]

Apparently he was an important personage or the son of a prominent family, for no king would elevate a nobody to such a high place as Ahasuerus raised Haman.

Can you see him sweeping along the palace halls, every flunky bowing and scraping before him—and at the king's command? From a later glimpse into his character, we can

1. *International Standard Bible Encyclopedia,* 2:1324.

assume that Haman ate this up. He was all the more infuriated, then, when his eye caught one man who dared to stand up straight on his two feet as the great Haman passed by. "Mordecai bowed not, nor did him reverence" (3:2).

THE COURAGE OF CONVICTION

Mordecai was not being boorish; not setting himself up as too proud to join the others who kowtowed to Haman. No! Mordecai was a Jew. He bowed only to his God. Like Daniel, his loyalty to God meant more than the favor of men, even of kings. Like Peter and John (Acts 4), he chose to obey God rather than man when the choice had to be made. Like many in every generation who dare to put God first whatever the cost, Mordecai was a man of principles, and he was willing to put himself on the line for them; this is the proof of sincerity.

Sometimes as Christians we have to do the same today. It may mean saying no when doing so will mark us a party-pooper, a square, or a wet blanket, but that is a lesser price to pay than violating our Christian conscience! It may mean taking a stand for Christ when it would be more comfortable to stay neutral. But we have His promise, "Whosoever shall confess me . . . shall [I] also confess" (Luke 12:8).

While for the time being, Mordecai had instructed his foster daughter not to reveal her Jewish heritage, he himself made no secret that he was a Jew.

Any person who will dare to be different is certain to be called in question; so, a day or two later, the king's courtiers began to make an issue of Mordecai's unusual conduct. They were not necessarily evil-intentioned—nor is everyone who tries to get a Christian to "be less of a fanatic."

The king's servants apparently did their best to get Mordecai to conform before they tattled to Haman. Perhaps their talk to Mordecai went something like this:

"Man! Don't you know the *king* set Haman up?"

"D'you want to lose your head, or something?"

"So, you *are* religious. But does religion have to enter into your everyday life? You must be some kind of a fanatic."

None of their talk affected Mordecai's fixed standard. We might question What maintained his zeal? For although God was working out His providential purposes in the lives of the Jewish people, it is safe to assume that these Jews would not be permitted to carry on their daily sacrifices and observe their feasts—the virtual heart of their religion. Without their temple worship and outward observances, only the staunchest would retain their zeal.

Not only in Shushan, but in many places through the centuries, God's people have been in positions where open fellowship and teaching of His Word has been denied them. Notable in this generation are those in the iron and bamboo curtained countries, and, most recently, our own prisoners of war in Vietnam. Said Col. Robinson Risner, a fighter pilot shot down in 1966, "I couldn't have made it if it wasn't for Jesus Christ, and being able to look up and see Him in some of the trying times."

Major Norman McDaniel stated, "There was at all times a desire to worship God. Sometimes individually, sometimes as a group, and men drew strength from this. Many of the men knew verses from the Bible and as these were shared [written on toilet paper with a blue liquid medicine], we were able to compile a good knowledge of the Bible."

I cannot think of a better reason for hiding God's Word in our heart, can you? Who can tell what the future holds, and how precious may be the Bible verses we store away against some famine.

Speaking at the Evangelical Press Association Convention (May 1973) Lt. Col. Abel added a note about the hymns the POWs sang. Their favorites, he recalled, were "Holy, Holy, Holy" and "When We All Get to Heaven."[2]

How blessed we are with our freedom to assemble, to read

2. Evangelical Press News Service, Feb. 17, 1973.

God's Word, to pray and sing, and to share our faith. But for this one man and Haman's later malicious reference to this Jew's law-keeping, we would have nothing to indicate that the book of Esther is a record of God's sovereign dealings with His people.

When Mordecai would not heed their suggestions that he join in bowing to Haman, the servants carried the story to the proud Haman, being careful to make something of the fact that Mordecai was a Jew.

Alerted, Haman took particular notice and caught Mordecai "neither bowing nor kneeling." And, "When Haman saw that Mordecai neither bowed nor knelt, he swelled up with anger, but he considered it beneath him to apprehend Mordecai singly, for they had told him of Mordecai's nationality, and he intended to destroy all the Jews, Mordecai's people, in all the realm of Ahasuerus" (3:5-6, Berkeley).

Was all this swelled up anger due solely to Mordecai's refusal to revere Haman, or were there others in this minority group who irked Haman to the point of raising his blood pressure? Whether or not, here was his chance to rid himself of a daily annoyance.

So the pogrom is plotted. But plans had to be timed auspiciously, and for guidance Haman resorted to "the lot" (3:7).

Had Haman never heard of the Pharaoh who likewise designed the extermination of the Hebrews? (Had not Nasser, when he threatened to drive the Israelis into the sea?)

The devious character of Haman comes out as we listen in on his portrayal of the so-called facts to the king. Like many before him and since, Haman skillfully twists the case so that he puts himself in the light of a champion looking out for the king's own interests. Hear his I'm-telling-you-for-your-own-good approach, a despicable device employed when one has an ax to grind.

"There is a certain people . . . in all the provinces of thy kingdom . . . it is not for the king's profit to suffer them"

(3:8). (A New Testament counterpart is found in Acts 16:20-21.) We might speculate as to which of the Jewish laws these Shushan Jews adhered to. The Sabbath? Their dietary laws? Their nonmixed marriage? Surely they would never bow to the idols of a pagan country.

Whatever their practices, Haman capitalized on their difference. Not a word to indicate that this is a personal vendetta; a revenge play by a man whose ego is badly bruised. A great king would scarcely be interested in such a petty problem.

One thing we cannot pass over without mentioning. Haman is willing to put his money where his mouth is. No modern politician jockeying for a position in Washington, Ottawa, London, or any other capital has been more willing to shoulder the financial burden. And it was not peanuts. You cannot exterminate a whole race of people scattered abroad in many areas without investing great sums of money in the venture. The cost of storm troopers, their transportation, and deadly equipment comes high in any age.

"I will pay twenty million silver dollars," Haman offered (3:9, Berkeley).

King Ahasuerus was unimpressed with the financial bribe. His treasury was not threatened by the needed outlay of funds to rid his world of the Jewish people. But we cannot pin a medal on him for his disinterest in the bribe. He was likewise indifferent to the heinous proposal Haman made that the Jews be disposed of. It is difficult to conceive of such callousness even in a king of that day.

Wholesale genocide was the issue. This generation has seen the near genocide of people in Biafra and again in Bangladesh. Men's hearts are as wicked in one era as another.

"Do with them as you please." King Ahasuerus dismissed the matter. Do we see in him a prophetic glimpse of one who in a later day would wash his hands and say concerning the fate of the King of the Jews, "See ye to it," (Matthew 27:24)?

What if the fate of the Jews had been left in Haman's hands!

At this point things could not have looked blacker for the Jews of Shushan and those all over the empire. Haman, however, was not reckoning on a Jewish queen's intervention.

Again, a letter-writing campaign is instituted, in the king's name (3:12). In obedience to Haman's summons, the royal scribes come running on that thirteenth day of the month Nisan.

Nothing was left to possible misinterpretation. The official edict sentencing a people to death was written in the dialect of each locality.

What thoughts went through the head of the mighty monarch as he turned over his signet ring—the seal of sovereignty—to the evil Haman? Did the king for one moment ponder what awesome power he was relegating to an underling—power which in Haman's hands became diabolical? Ahasuerus could have won for himself a place in the annals of history as a great champion of justice and example of compassion.

Malicious and cruel as Haman was, he could have had no power to implement his infamous scheme unless such power were given him by the king.

The speedy riders are on their way bearing the irrevocable decree—the law of the Medes and Persians that altereth not. No options are open to the deputies in the provinces; the order was the same the empire over. How did it read?

> The letters were sent by swift posts to all the royal provinces, to wipe out, to kill, and to destroy all the Jews, young and old, children and women, in one day the thirteenth of the twelfth month (3:13, Berkeley).

It was a mammoth undertaking arranging to notify every country in the realm. But at last the tireless Haman heaved a pleasant sigh of relief. The deed was as good as done.

Then "the king and Haman sat down to drink" (3:15). Can you believe it! Human callousness was unmatched again until time would change from B.C. to A.D. and some soldiers would gamble at the foot of a cross.

But neither the king nor his henchman Haman reflected the attitude of the Persian people in Shushan. The pogrom against the Jews gave no cause for celebration to them. The Jewish captives had made friends in their captivity. The grief of the stricken, doomed people was shared by many of the Medes and Persians (somewhat restoring our faith in human nature).

We too would join them in their despair except that it has been given to us to know the end of this story, to know that the last word was not Haman's.

God's master plan called for a *Jewish* maiden to be the mother of the Saviour of all mankind. The Jews *must* survive until that prophecy be fulfilled, Haman or a thousand Hamans!

The Jewish race *will* survive until God winds up His clock for the last time, and "no weapon that is formed against them will prosper."

To Think About and Do

1. It would be understandable that Mordecai would be interested in preventing the assassination of Esther's husband. But Mordecai had not revealed his relationship to the new queen. What if he had not been at the right place at the right time, or if, in possession of the knowledge, he had decided it was safer not to get involved.

2. How does Mordecai's attitude and action contrast with much of society's callousness in our own day? What New Testament principle is involved? (See Luke 10:30-37.)

3. Can you pinpoint something important in your own life that occurred because you were in the right place at the right time? Share such an incident with newer Christians, helping them, too, to trace God's hand on their lives.

4. What might have sustained Mordecai, the Jew, in a pagan society? From the marginal references in Genesis 28:15, find additional promises to those who are the victims of persecution; read Psalm 37, marking the "fret not's." Discuss their significance. As Christians, our sustenance can be found in such verses as Matthew 5:10; 2 Timothy

1:12; Hebrews 13:5. Of profound value against the day of persecution is our *memorizing* Romans 8:28, 38-39.

5. For the most part we know nothing of suffering for Christ, but when it does come, how willing are we to stand up for what we believe, and confess Christ openly, even though it marks us as different?

6. What approach did Haman use to ingratiate himself with the king and assure that his scheme would win the king's approval?

7. Why was it not enough for Haman to rid himself of Mordecai—why the whole Jewish race?

8. How much responsibility must the king accept for the evil plot? We might ask ourselves, Am I to any degree prejudiced toward another race or nationality? Would I put my own safety on the line to stand up for their rights, or am I morally indifferent?

9. What does the utter callousness of Haman and the king remind you of?

10. Why could Haman's plan never succeed?

11. This week, play the exciting game of finding God's hand in seemingly little things in your life. No day can then be dull and meaningless; rather, moment by moment you will feel God's nearness, and you will sense that you, like Esther, are playing a vital role in God's overall plan.

4

The Queen at the Crossroads

All the world knows that anyone . . . who goes into the king's inner court without his summons is doomed to die unless the king holds out his golden scepter (4:11, TLB).

Read Esther 4:1-14

Callousness incarnate. A city in confusion. Such was the scene in Shushan. The posts, the carriers of the dread writ against the Jews, likewise broadcast terror wherever their grim mission took them.

God could have elected to move in and deliver His doomed people by means of a miracle. He chose rather, as He frequently does, to use people.

MORDECAI IN MOURNING

It is understandable that Mordecai would feel some inner pressure to do something in the situation. Was he not in a sense responsible for the dire predicament of his people? Was it not his personal failure to kowtow to the newly promoted Haman that had incensed the proud official and triggered the diabolical plot to exterminate the Jews?

No impulsive activist, Mordecai "ascertained everything that had been done" (4:1, Berkeley). He was not about to react to some idle rumor. But, the enormity of the impending disaster verified, he did what Jews through the centuries had done when

33

mourning was called for: he donned sackcloth, the coarse cloth of goat's hair made into a sacklike garment. And he lamented loudly in the streets. Doubtless, mingled with his despair was a certain amount of guilt for his part in inciting Haman. But no true Jew was going to bow to any save Jehovah! Possibly Mordecai could have spared himself the remorse if such troubled him, for men like Haman will always find some excuse to seemingly justify their vindictiveness.

Mordecai's greater interest was, "What can I do to stop the pogrom from being carried out?"

THE CRIME? BEING JEWISH

We have no record of what the decree actually spelled out beyond the awful fact itself: "To destroy, to kill, and to cause to perish all Jews . . . upon the thirteenth day of the twelfth month . . . and to take the spoil" (3:13). How were the various communities and countries supposed to go about accomplishing this decree? Would they cause all Jews to register (or had they already done that as a matter of course)? Or would they rely upon their ability to recognize a Jewish person on sight? Many Jews are easily categorized by their facial features. In fact, because of this very identifiableness, some Jewish parents have reluctantly had plastic surgery performed on their children in an effort to guard against further Hitlerism. The often joked-about nose job is no laugh to some Jewish people. It is a defense mechanism for survival.

It is difficult for those of us who have never experienced the midnight knock, the rude dragging away of son or father never to be seen alive again, to empathize with those who have gone through such agony. Their crime? Being Jewish, like the family of Anne Frank, and those harbored by compassionate Christians like Corrie Ten Boom.

In the spring of 1972, it was my privilege to visit Bangladesh while that nation was still reeling from the war for independence. With my daughter, a missionary nurse in that country, and other missionaries, I was invited into the homes of a number of Hindu Bengalis. Not only did they relate some of their horrifying experiences, they also reenacted them for us. The tramp-tramp of army boots, the sharp knock (or no knock), the merciless interrogation, "Where are your daughters?" and the dragging away of the son or the father, or both. Their crime? They were *Hindus*.

So must have been the horror in every town and hamlet when the king's decree reached the Jewish people.

THE LAST ONE TO HEAR THE BAD NEWS

In the security of the palace, the queen must have been among the last in Shushan to be informed of the plot. Had the servants sought to spare her such tidings as royalty need not be troubled by hearing? They could not know its intense meaning for their queen. Who among them even dreamed that she was one of the doomed race?

Actually, not the news of the impending evil, but just the matter of Mordecai's being garbed in mourning reached her at first. Shocked over this tale of Mordecai in sackcloth, she took immediate action. She must have been aware of the prohibition against anyone dressed in such clothes entering the royal gate. So she sent a new suit to her foster father. Was it her intent that he would then hurry and personally acquaint her with the reason for the garments of mourning? Or was some of the materialism of a pagan court rubbing off on her, and did she think that a suit of clothes would fix up whatever was occasioning Mordecai's actions?

Her offer was rejected.

More concerned now, Esther sent the trusted Hatach to find out for her, from Mordecai himself "the what and wherefore of it" (4:5, Berkeley).

Mordecai spared no details as to why he was in sackcloth. For verification he sent to Esther a copy of the written edict then, as though to lend graphic reality to the report, he added

an account of the exact sum of money Haman had offered to
put up to finance the wholesale slaughter.

Why would Mordecai consider it important at this time that
Esther be aware of Haman's part? Surely it was not a way of
getting some slight revenge by demeaning Haman in Esther's
eyes. The national, racial stakes were too high to permit of
personal feuding. It would seem that Mordecai, a farseeing
man as has been evidenced, realized that Esther would view
Haman as the man whom the king had seen fit to elevate above
all the other court members: just that. And the wise Mordecai
thus warns Esther of the kind of person she may sometime
have dealings with in the palace. Also, it is the height of strategy to *know your enemy*.

IT IS UP TO YOU, ESTHER!

To Queen Esther, Hatach's news brought more than grief.
It brought soul-searching, for Mordecai had laid on her shoulders a burden too great to contemplate. Call on the king!
Beg for his mercy and plead for her people! Well did Esther
know the probable price to herself: death.

Back went the messenger Hatach with her answer.

"All the king's courtiers and all the residents in the provinces
know that for every person, man or woman, who enters the
king's inner court uninvited, there is one penalty, execution"
(4:11, Berkeley), and she went on to add that for thirty days
she had not been called by the king into his presence. Her
reply to Mordecai's suggestion is neither consent nor refusal;
it is a reasonable explanation of the danger involved and a
bid for understanding of her position. In effect she is saying,
"I know I'm the queen, but that doesn't give me the privileges
you're talking about. The king has a whole harem at his beck
and call—and it's been a whole month since he has asked to
see me." There is something of the child pleading with her
father, even though Esther is queen of the realm.

We might question his right to make such demands of Esther, unless we recognize that he was a man of unusual insight and apparently was specially guided. Also, his people and their fate were of primary concern to him.

Understandably, then, his response to Esther's message came speedily. Almost brutally he came to the point: "Do not imagine that because you are inside the royal palace, you alone of all the Jews will escape." (What kind of a life would that be? The question is inherent in his threat.)

Then, loud and clear rings out the belief of this man who knows the God of history; he knows that God has a plan and that this plan is inextricably entwined with the promises to Israel.

"Delivery and rescue will come," he declares unequivocally. If not through Esther, it will come from another source. And Mordecai goes on to enunciate a principle that applies in every age: While evil may prevail because good people sit still, keep quiet, and do nothing, nevertheless these good people suffer with the rest when the trouble comes.

The deliverance will come—but Esther and her family with her will be destroyed.

Esther could be pardoned for rationalizing, "I can be a loser whichever way I decide."

Climaxing Mordecai's plea—warning—threat—is the challenge of the ages. "And who knows whether you have come to the kingdom for such a time as this?"

It was a personal challenge directed only at Queen Esther. "Who knows if *you* are come to the kingdom? *You* are the privileged one, and privilege brings responsibility. You, Esther, are the one in a position to effect change. You have your people in your hands. You—you—you—not somebody else."

GOD HAS NO SMALL JOBS

Like Queen Esther, we too are privileged. As God's redeemed people, we have been elevated into membership in heaven's royal family. And, like Esther, we have responsibilities as a direct result of privilege. Often this may entail forgetting our selfish plans in the interest of serving God and our fellow man. Jesus said, "Whosoever will come after me, let him deny himself, and take up his cross, and follow me" (Mark 8:34b).

Then there is Paul's reference to our reasonable service: "I plead with you to give your bodies to God. Let them be a living sacrifice, holy—the kind He can accept. When you think of what He has done for you, is this too much to ask?" (Romans 12:1, TLB).

In every age, in every level of society, privilege carries with it the tacit assumption of responsibility.

Sometimes we fail to do what is obviously in our path for us to do. Because it is not a big, important thing, we may pass it up, thinking, *If it were something significant and challenging God was asking me to do, that would be different. I believe I would rise to such a challenge.* But does not that savor of the person who says. "If only I had a million dollars, what wonderful things I could do for the Lord's work." The credibility of that statement is in how much the person is doing with such finances as God has trusted him with in the present. The great humanitarian, John D. Rockefeller, was asked, "Don't you find it hard to give away such large sums of money?"

"I might," said this benefactor, "except that when I earned my first dollar, I was careful to set aside a tenth for God."

It was the widow who gave *out of her poverty* whom Jesus immortalized, (Luke 21:3). And, according to the Scriptures, the way up the ladder of stewardship success is being faithful when we are still at the bottom (Luke 19:17).

God has no small jobs. Moreover, God has certain explicit expectations of us as believers. He expects us to be His witnesses (Matthew 5:16; Acts 1:8); He expects us to display certain attitudes such as being *loving*, and *forgiving* (Matthew 19:19; Luke 6:37; Romans 13:8; Ephesians 4:32; 1 John 3:11; 4:19). These are directives, not electives of the Christian life.

BUT WHAT ABOUT ME?

In his directive to Esther, Mordecai had made no mention of the personal danger if she should follow through with his suggestion. He had been careful to pinpoint what would happen to her and her people if she failed to plead with the king for their deliverance. But there was the other side. Perhaps Esther had dropped hints about the possibility of someone in the court approaching the king for this purpose. "Better to keep out of it," would have been the strong advice to such a person.

Certain death for all the Jews if she were to keep still.

Almost certain death for herself if she were to do as her foster father bade her.

And then—that part about "coming to the kingdom for such a time as this"! Could it be? Was it for this she had been elevated to the throne?

Was ever a young woman at such a crossroads?

TO THINK ABOUT AND DO

1. In your opinion, to what extent was Mordecai responsible for the plight of his people? What alternatives (if any) did he have in his attitude toward Haman?
2. How far are you willing to go when your principles are jeopardized? Think of a specific personal instance. In retrospect, do you feel good inside about how you acted in the situation, or do you wish you had done differently?
3. If you had been in Esther's shoes, would you have wished to be kept in the dark? Why? Why not?
4. What are your thoughts concerning Mordecai's right to ask such a sacrifice of Esther? What primarily motivated him?
5. How reasonable were Esther's arguments as to why she should not become involved as Mordecai had told her she should?
6. From what we have learned about Mordecai thus far, would you figure that it was faith that made him declare

deliverance would come? Or, was there an element of pressuring Esther in this assertion?

7. You and I will never be asked or required to do what confronted Esther. Since some of us are prone to think, *God would never use me for something big and important*, how does this affect your willingness to do what you consider small and unimportant? What reasons or excuses would you give to God for your bypassing such opportunities?

8. Discuss how we are empowered, enabled, and motivated to do the things God expects us to do as believers (Matthew 28:18; Luke 23:34; 2 Corinthians 5:14). With the help of a concordance find additional verses on this theme.

9. Think of a circumstance when you almost passed up a small job for God, then reconsidered—with joyful results.

If you feel that you have failed to rise to the big or little challenges God has given you, do not let such feelings crush you and make you feel like a failure. Tell God all about it. He delights in helping us up and giving us another chance. All it takes is for us to want to be His "certain person" in the right place at the right time.

Each of us comes to some "kingdom" for a particular time. There *is* something that only *you* can do.

5

If I Perish, I Perish

Esther put on her royal robes and entered the inner court (5:1, TLB).

Read Esther 4:15—5:5

QUESTION OF THE AGES

Who knows if you are come to the kingdom for such a time as this?

Who knows? A question of the ages.

Esther did not know, that is for sure. Yet, in Mordecai's rhetorical question is bound up all the mind-boggling, near miraculous happenings that had brought her to her present position in the kingdom.

Who knows? The correct answer to the question did not automatically give her the grand prize as on a TV show.

Queen Esther. A flesh-and-blood woman with a Cinderella story—happy ending and all. Loving life, she was confronted with almost certain death.

We cannot possibly put ourselves in her place, for we know the end of the story. She did not.

We can be sure that her decision was not on the spur of the moment "I know what I'll do." It would only come after much agony of soul. It came. The messenger carried to Mordecai words that have echoed ever since:

"I will go . . . and if I perish, I perish" (4:16).

In all of literature there is no greater dramatic line.

But it is not for its literary worth we value Esther's announced decision.

There is faith in her *if*. There is also realism. For some do perish—in our day as in hers—when they put their lives on the line for other people or for God.

There is raw courage in her decision. For this is courage, to know the danger and to determine to face it whatever the cost. It does not take so much courage when we suddenly find ourselves in the midst of a situation that calls for brave action that we have no time to evaluate as to the possible consequences, or when we have no option.

PHASE ONE

All Esther's background and heritage are reflected in this moment of crisis. No longer is she the Jewess incognito. Not for her a possibly secure position in a pagan palace at the price of her silence as to her nationality! Such a choice is rarely made at the actual point of a moral crossroads. Rather, it has been forming out of the warp and woof of all that we are: our background, our heritage, our true character. The crossroad or crisis merely gives opportunity for us to demonstrate what we really are.

Mordecai need not have feared. He had done his work well as he raised her. Perhaps his demands of her only showed that he knew her better than she knew herself.

The crisis calls for extreme measures—fasting on the part of all the Jews that Mordecai could find in Shushan. The conditional clause in her consenting to Mordecai's dangerous assignment for her: three days and nights of fasting.

It is worth noting that Esther did not think of this as a "do-it-myself" project. Also, she is to be commended for including herself and those close to her in the stringent requirement she was imposing on all the other Jews in Shushan.

So—phase one of her plan called for fasting.

A whole volume could well be devoted to this subject that

seems far removed from practicality for many Christians. Perhaps we are not confronted with extremity frequently enough.

Jesus said to His disciples on one occasion, "If you have faith as a grain of mustard seed. . . . Howbeit this kind goeth not out but by prayer and fasting" (Matthew 17:20-21). They were failing in something Jesus had commissioned them to do (17:14-17), and He gave them the formula for success.

Jesus Himself fasted. And numerous outstanding events in the Old Testament are related to fasting.

Missionary friends tell a graphic incident of God's intervention after they set aside a day for prayer and fasting. A colleague had suffered a total mental collapse. Highly qualified missionaries on that field applied all their medical and psychiatric skill, devoting themselves to the beloved patient. The whole compound and many of the national believers prayed earnestly. But the handwriting appeared to be on the wall. The missionary must be flown to the states, where further care could be given in a hospital setting for such patients.

One missionary child held on to God in prayer, serenely sure of the outcome. A member of the group felt strangely led to call for a day of fasting. The others gladly cooperated, although it was an uncommon thing to ask. The outcome? God honored their *prayer* and *fasting*. The patient came back to reality. Every test the doctors could apply verified that God had healed their colleague. The trip to the states was cancelled. A whole family was spared the anguished uprooting from their service for the Lord. And God was magnified in the eyes of all who knew and heard of the miracle.

Certainly God never makes suggestions which are not beneficial to us when we carry them out.

Perhaps we should say a word about a possible negative aspect of the practice of fasting. Jesus deplored the *attitude* of the Pharisees with regard to fasting (Matthew 6:16). Nevertheless, He said "when" not "if" you fast.

There is not one word to indicate that Esther (or Mordecai,

for that matter) *prayed*. But would they separate prayer and fasting?

Because it was important to her, critical in fact, Esther issued her request, and she herself and her personal servants fasted likewise. What can we read into this? "So Mordecai went his way, and did according to all that Esther had commanded him" (4:17).

DRESSED FOR THE OCCASION

It was not just the woman in her that made Esther get all dressed up in her robes of royalty while the rest of her people wore sackcloth. For one thing, had she joined them in wearing the garb of mourning, where would it have gotten her (see 4:2)? Second, it was fitting that she should wear her best when she was to seek an audience with the king, proving her high regard for him.

There might have been still another reason, and with this one almost any woman will empathize. It is this: the sense that we are dressed just right for a particular occasion gives us a poise. We then can dismiss any feelings of apprehension as to whether we are looking all right; looking our best, and we can concentrate on what we are supposed to be concentrating on. Here is an example.

I was shopping in a big department store in Pasadena, and I met a friend who, I knew, had been invited to speak at an important conference. "Are you all set for the conference?" I asked.

"Well, not quite," she said. Then, holding out a bulky box, "But I've just gotten my *dress*. Now that that's settled, I can get to my speech," she added in a breezy manner.

I understood what she meant. Sometimes I have suffered after I arrived for a speaking engagement, wondering, "Should I have worn something else?" when I really needed to keep my mind on my message; on my purpose for being where I was. And this is not vanity. The fact is that a woman (and, I suspect, a man too) projects best when he feels confident that he looks his best.

Esther need have no qualms on that score. She was dressed fit for a king.

WHEN GOD SAYS, "GO"

Dressed in her finery, Esther was nevertheless on a collision course with the law, and the penalty for that was death.

What would some of her thoughts be as she stepped from her queenly apartments? Perhaps, *How can I ever tell Ahasuerus that I am Jewish?* Certainly she must have been obsessed with the ultimate fear, "Will he not even let me *speak* to him? Will he just order my execution?"

Her fears were unfounded. But how different it might have been. Suppose some lesser courtier had seen her approach and had taken things into his own hands, thinking he was carrying out the law. Haman did not know her nationality, so he was not out to get her. But, if he had been there at the time, he could have drawn the king's attention to the fact that the queen had come unbidden. Haman had influenced the king before, with dire results as we know.

But no. Esther stood in the inner court of the king's house. And the king sat on his throne. "And it was so, when the king saw Esther the queen standing in the court, that she obtained favour in his sight" (5:2).

Phase one was going well at the start. But Esther would never have known how the king would react, if she had not daringly made the first move. Sometimes we tend to excuse ourselves for our inaction by saying, "I mustn't run ahead of God," when actually we are lagging behind.

Can you hear Esther's sigh of relief—a sigh that was to be heard all over the area of Shushan, for surely Mordecai had established some sure means of knowing how Esther did.

The king's gracious gesture of extending his golden sceptre was her sign that she had obtained favor.

Perhaps you can think of a time when you felt constrained, almost compelled, to go somewhere, do something that was very difficult for you to do. But the Holy Spirit would not let you excuse yourself. And you straightened your shoulders— and went. And ever since, you have been amazed and delighted at the way things went. It might have been, as has been my own experience, going only because you could not shake the conviction that you must, to the home of an unsaved person who had shown only hostility toward the gospel—and toward you. But that was God's time, and in His providence you were His person for such a time—and God worked on both ends of the situation. When this is so, the result cannot but be beautiful.

This Esther found. Whether the fasting had paid off, we cannot tell. But so far, she was safe.

PHASE TWO

During the three days and nights when she and her people had but one concern—survival—Esther had formulated a plan. In this we recognize her to be not only beautiful but wise. We do not read that she had any advisors surrounding her. Apparently she had not seen even Mordecai in the intervening days.

She drew near and touched the top of the sceptre that was in her husband's hand. This would teach us that it takes two, one to offer and the other to accept, in order for plans to go forward.

Her wisdom likewise comes through in that she held back from rushing and falling at the king's feet and spilling out the problem and her personal grief. With such an offer as the king made, it must have been hard not to rush in.

This monarch knew well that Esther's was no social call, no wifely stop at his office. Life and death were involved, literally. He, with a wave of his sceptre, nullified the decree that would have been against her for coming unbidden. But his curiosity was doubtless aroused. He did not bother with the customary long, drawn-out amenities of the East. He asked the straightforward question, "What can I do for you?" And before he could know what he was committing himself to, he added, "It shall be given you to the half of my kingdom." And it was no idle promise. He could fulfill it, and no one could stop him.

Her request. Does it seem trivial—capricious almost? Oh, but Esther knew what she was doing. She was setting the stage for her supreme appeal.

The scene ends with the king ordering Haman to present himself at Esther's banquet, at *Esther's* request. Esther, the Jewess. Esther, woman of destiny. Haman is in for a surprise!

To Think About and Do

In every century, God has His Esther, His Mordecai, His man and woman who do not bow to the seemingly inevitable; who count not their lives dear unto themselves. Trusting God, they defy circumstances, and accomplish exploits for Him, in spite of the Ahasueruses and the Hamans. So we can take heart in our troubled times.

1. List the pros and cons that must have influenced Esther's decision. What factors guide you in a decision that involves some personal sacrifice? Whatever our need for guidance, the ultimate guidance factor is the Lord Himself. He has promised "I will guide thee" (Psalm 32:8). God uses His Word, His Holy Spirit indwelling each believer (John 16:13-14), and many times He uses people and circumstances. Here is a little guidance tip: God's guidance will always square with what He says in His Word. Beware of any "spiritual guidance" that is contrary to the Bible. Share some inspiring instance of God's guidance, your own experience or that of someone you know.

2. What proves that Esther was a woman of unusual courage?

3. Why do you think that fasting was such a major factor in her agreeing to the dangerous assignment? What did she

hope it would accomplish? With the help of a concordance, locate the word *fasting* in both the Old and the New Testaments. Study the portions carefully and consider: the stated reason for the fasting; the given result of fasting; your own honest attitudes on the subject.

4. Do you think the writer is placing undue emphasis on Esther's being appropriately dressed for the occasion? Why or why not? How important is it to you that you appear at your best, as a Christian representing our Lord?

5. How much is Esther's selfless determination going to influence you to be more daring for God, especially as you realize that God had worked on the king's heart at the same time?

6. What lessons of wise procedure can we learn from studying Esther's strategy and preparation? How does it relate to our seeking an audience with the King of kings?

6

Party with a Purpose

Now tell me what you really want, and I will give it to you, even if it is half of the kingdom (5:6, TLB).

Read Esther 5:6-14

WHAT ARE YOU WAITING FOR, ESTHER?

Back in her royal suite, was Esther down on her knees thanking God for the success of her undertaking thus far? That she had not anticipated failure is borne out by one statement she made to the king: "Come to the banquet I have prepared." There was no hint of, "If you will accept my invitation, I will prepare." Oh no! And what a lesson this can be to some of us who are of little faith. Sometimes we come to God with an urgent and important request, something that can only come to pass if He will intervene for us, and then we proceed on the assumption that He will not hear us, not grant our petition. Esther was the kind of person we could expect to carry an umbrella along to a prayer meeting convened to pray for rain in a time of severe drought.

Successful as her venture was, are you perhaps thinking, *Why didn't she make the most of her grand opportunity? I know what I would have done in her place.* So do I. I would likely have spilled out the whole story. But, are you familiar with the verse that reads, "He that believeth shall not make haste" (Isaiah 28:16b)?'

The Bible also tells us that there is a time for everything. To you and me, the time for Esther's appeal would seem to have been that point at which the king graciously received her and allayed her fears. Esther must have felt otherwise.

We can take comfort in the fact that time was still on her side. You will recall that while the decree was issued on the thirteenth of the first month, it was to be enforced on the thirteenth of the twelfth month. Haman had made provision for the news to reach into the remotest corners of the empire, and then the wholesale slaughter would be carried out all on the same day. No chance for pockets of resistance to survive. No guerrilla bands to harass him later on. Complete extermination was his program, and that called for organization, strategy, and time.

WHEN THE TIME IS RIGHT

Esther had something in mind, we can be sure. She would sense the propitious moment for her purpose. We can all understand such a situation. Though our requests would pale beside Esther's, nevertheless they have been important to us at the time. Even a child has a feeling for the right time when he would ask Mother or Dad for something special. An employee senses when the time is right to broach the subject of a salary raise, when the employer is in a mellow mood and when conditions are right. He would not risk asking before then and risk blowing his chances.

We have to grant to Esther that she was waiting for the right time. We do not know whether Mordecai had been able to slip notes to her, making suggestions. It would be reasonable to assume that during the long hours of fasting and waiting, God had revealed to her His plan. I know a missionary who, as a fledgling appointee, faced the (to him) ordeal of a missionary conference where he would be expected to speak many times. He was in a state of near panic as he journeyed by train across the states to that conference. But as he prayed, he felt led to fast, wait on God, and read his Bible. He relates that as he did so, a calm came over him. Before long he saw in his mind's eye a clear-cut outline of the manner in which he should present his mission field and challenge the hearts of his listeners. He could hardly wait. And those who attended that conference and heard this missionary appointee have never forgotten his organized, creative presentation.

In such a way, God may have revealed to Esther His procedure for her to follow. Certainly God did not place her in her strategic position, with an incredible weight on her young shoulders, and then abandon her. Nor would He be likely to leave the fate of His chosen people to her untried wisdom.

This girl Esther was no Joan of Arc. She had no army with her riding at its head, nor did she claim to hear voices. Her role had been determined the day she was chosen by a pagan king to be his queen, which undoubtedly was an act of God.

Now she awaited the fateful meeting with the king and his prime minister.

PHASE THREE

The two men arrive. Again the king makes an opening for her to speak her heart, with his kindly question and his repeated offer to grant her up to the half of the kingdom. Surely now she will speak, tell what had motivated her to risk her life the previous day. But again she parries the king's question with one of her own. We might ask What more does she want? Was she being capricious? No, the stakes were too high for that. But what if the king had countered with, "Oh, no! I've given you two chances. I've made you the most attractive offer any woman could ever be given. No more playing games with me."

Esther apparently had no such fears that he would become impatient or angry with her and that she would blow her chance. The second time she issued her invitation to a banquet. She must have felt that phase three was the right procedure in her desperate efforts to save her people. And the king must have loved her very much. How else can we view his present

tolerance in the light of his treatment of Vashti, Esther's prede-
cessor? Did he sense that he was not dealing with a woman's
whim?

Something unusual must have impressed him. Why else
would he restrain what would have been pardonable impatience
with this wife of his? It could be that in her hours alone and
fasting, an even greater beauty had been given her, an inner
spirituality that glowed radiantly on the outside. The apoch-
ryphal chapters of Esther speak of her calling upon God in
desperation for her people, reminding God that they were His
people.

The king heard Esther out, and amazingly he acceded to
her requests without demur or demand for an explanation. And
this time she did promise to reveal her request "tomorrow."

TRUE TO CHARACTER

What about Haman? Can you see him strutting through the
palace, gloating over his favor with the queen? Haman may
never have heard that pride goeth before destruction, and a
haughty spirit before a fall (Pr 16:18), but he was to experience it!

The Bible has much to say about pride. Nebuchadnezzar is
a classic example of the folly of pride. His colossal pride cli-
maxed in his having an image built to himself (Daniel 3:1-7).
The story of the incredible results reads like bestseller fiction
(but it is not fiction!) Then, in Daniel 4:37, now in his right
mind, this great king proclaims, "Those that walk in pride he
[the King of heaven] is able to abase."

You and I are not likely to be guilty of such blatant pride,
nor of having such dramatic consequences in our lives, but
pride is an insidious sin that snares most of us at some time.
And God hates pride. In fact, "A proud look" heads the list
of the seven things the Lord hates (Proverbs 6:17-18, see
21:4). Then, in case we might be tempted to think that only
the Old Testament concerns itself with sinful pride, the practi-

cal James tells us that "God resisteth the proud, but giveth grace unto the humble" (James 4:6).

We hear the saying, "proud as Lucifer:" that was the ultimate sin; it drove Satan from his high place. And today pride can make people unreasonable. Pride in material possessions; pride in our superior intellect; pride in our position in life; even undue pride in our children that makes us forget that *all* we have, in whatever area of life, is solely because of God's goodness, grace, and favor toward us. This realization makes us humbly grateful and puts us in line for the grace James talks about.

Let us rejoin Haman on his proud walk home. "The queen's favorite, next to the king himself," he may have been thinking. Two invitations in a row, and for him alone besides the king! His elation was short-lived, though, for, in the place where we have come to expect him to be, was Mordecai the Jew. And he was not kneeling; not bowing and scraping; not kowtowing to Haman.

The black hatred that had sparked the plot against the Jews flared up again, blotting out the gladness Haman had been feeling. He is living up to the character he has displayed thus far: arrogant, demanding center stage and adulation. The procuring of a death-dealing decree against a nation had not availed to cool the personal vendetta with Mordecai. All it took to arouse Haman's fury was Mordecai calmly ignoring him. Forgotten for the moment is the pride and the glory that was his in the king's court, so devastating to his ego was this one man's refusal to bow to him.

He recovers his equilibrium, however, as he ponders on all he has to brag about when he reaches his home. And brag he does! He brags about the glory of his riches, about his children, about his promotion by the king, and about the queen's honoring him by inviting him along with the king, to her banquet (5:12).

Doubtless his wife and his friends all gathered around to

congratulate him on his good fortune. And he most likely ate it
up. It was fitting that they should rejoice with him, for as he
related the tale, it was something to rejoice about. There is
nothing wrong with rejoicing with those who do rejoice, as the
Scriptures enjoin us. (Sometimes we find it easier to weep with
those who weep!)

But right in the midst of the happy time, a black cloud
comes over Haman's face, and he changes from conqueror to
avenger. That hated Mordecai! He is a bone sticking in Haman's throat. Something has to be done to get rid of him. He
begins by baring his embittered heart as to what Mordecai did
and did not do. It would be easy to elicit empathy from his
friends. But it is his wife who is quick to offer a grisly solution.
Was she, we might ponder, willing that any price be paid just
so long as Haman could be mollified? What matter that an in-
nocent man would die a cruel death? And not only does she
advocate the hanging, but she further panders to Haman's small
soul by suggesting that this be a spectacle no one would miss:
a gallows seventy-five feet high would guarantee this (5:14,
Berkeley). Then, shades of "the king and Haman sat down to
drink" (3:15), this woman recomends that Haman "go . . . in
merrily with the king unto the banquet" (5:14)!

THE HAND OF GOD IN THE GLOVE OF HUMAN EVENTS

With the economy of words we so often find in Scripture,
the reaction of Haman to this suggestion is recorded: "The
thing pleased Haman; and he caused the gallows to be made"
(5:14). We could have guessed that it would please him.

Where is Mordecai as this tall scaffold is being erected?
Seated at the gate, where we can reasonably expect he would
be, would Mordecai be among the first to hear any news coming
hot off the lips of those who carried it? Or, had Haman guar-
anteed that nothing would go amiss by arranging for Mordecai
to be picked up? If the would-be victim did know of his fate,
if perhaps he could hear the hammering of the carpenters build-

ing the gallows, what were his thoughts? Had he, like other heroes of the Bible and every century since, resolved that come what may he would not violate his conscience?

And what of Esther? There is nothing to indicate that, in the seclusion of her apartments, she was aware of the mortal threat to her kinsman—that is, apart from the immediate series of "coincidences." In reading and rereading and studying and again reading this seventeenth book of the Old Testament, I have been impressed that if all the coincidences from beginning to end were programmed into a computer, this input would possibly so boggle the mechanical brain that it would grind to a halt and scream for an operator (as a master technician tells me does happen to computers when faced with confusing data).

Dr. Vernon McGee calls such seeming coincidences "the hand of God in the glove of human events." Strange it is, then, that in this cliff-hanging drama, this phenomenal record of providential intervention, the name of God does not once appear.

MAN PROPOSES—GOD DISPOSES

As a veritable "king of the mountain" Haman leaves his wife to go and implement her diabolical proposal. Just one thread of hope hung betwen Mordecai and destruction: *the king had to give his consent.* So it is that Haman goes to have an audience with the king, very early in the morning. No doubt he feels that this is a mere formality. Has not Ahasuerus consented without a murmur to the plot to exterminate the whole Jewish race? Surely he will not now quibble about the execution of one Jew? And him a troublemaker at that.

But the curtain is about to rise on the next act in Shushan the palace. An evil man must be given enough rope to hang himself.

And Esther? In her mind did she often hear, "up to the half of my kingdom—up to the half of my kingdom"?

For Esther, half of the kingdom or the whole kingdom was

no panacea for the ills of her people. Half of the kingdom was no guarantee of the retraction of the death warrant.

Did Esther go to bed that night rehearsing how she might best frame her appeal to her husband, the emperor?

To Think About and Do

1. What evidence do we have of Esther's very special kind of faith in believing that her husband would receive her and give her a hearing? What New Testament characters demonstrated admirable faith? (See Mark 7:24-30; Luke 7:1-9).

2. Share with the group an instance when God gave you (or someone you know) such assurance in the face of overwhelming impossibilities?

3. How do you view Esther's putting off rather than grasping her opportunity of the moment? What circumstances might cause you to delay in making an important request? Recall an instance when you have proven delay to be for the best; when you have regretted your putting off. List the advantages of proper timing in carrying out a special project.

4. You doubtless believe that God does give specific guidance when we ask Him. Ask yourself, How willing am I to let other people be so led, without showing a sceptical or critical attitude toward this leading?

5. Sometimes, in drawing character sketches of other people, we emphasize defects in them that really point up our awareness of our own weaknesses and sins. If you were doing a character sketch of Haman, what would you emphasize? Should honesty cause you to admit to being proud and boastful, how willing are you to let God search your heart on this matter? In what do you take undue pride, and how does this affect your relationships with other people? What steps are you planning to take to change— this very week?

6. Why (according to Mordecai's insightful warning) was half of the kingdom valueless to Esther?

7

Flashback—The King Who Could Not Sleep

He came across the item telling how . . . two . . .
watchmen at the palace gates . . . had plotted to
assassinate him (6:1, TLB).

Read Esther 6:1-14

If we would doubt that the book of Esther is other than a re-counting of God's providential dealings, all we need do is read this sixth chapter. So much—so incredibly much—hinged on what is so simply stated: "On that night could not the king sleep."

A king could not sleep. Doubtless many kings, and queens too, have had sleepless nights, but this has not been matter for historical record. What makes this king's inability to sleep of paramount importance? The timing.

"On that night could not the king sleep," the record goes (6:1). On what night? The night on which his man, Haman, had devised a scheme to rid himself once and for all of Mordecai, the Jew. All Haman needed to implement his plan was the king's consent, and that appeared to be a foregone conclusion in Haman's mind. Had not the king gone along with his plot to wipe out all the Jews in his empire?

A sleepless night. Did not the sophisticated Persian culture boast of sleeping potions? If this king had lived in our time, the solution to his problem would have been as close as the nearest all-night drugstore.

Even commoners have certain alternatives when we cannot sleep. We can read; we can get a glass of warm milk; even counting blessings or saying Bible verses can be effective sleep inducers.

As king, Ahasuerus had everything going for him. He could have commanded the court physician to prescribe for his insomnia; he could have ordered his favorite food or drink or entertainment to while away his sleepless hours. (Like the legendary Ol' King Cole, he could have "called for his fiddlers three" to play soothing music. King Saul requisioned David to soothe his troubled spirits with harp strains in 1 Samuel 16:23).

But no! God's plan for His people called for a different solution to the king's sleep problem.

Totally unaware of his part in God's long-range plan, the king chose to regale himself with the recital of the history of his own times.

WHY WAS THE KING UNABLE TO SLEEP?

Have you found yourself speculating as to why this monarch could not sleep? We all have occasional bouts of wakefulness; sometimes we can trace the cause, and other times we cannot. What would make Ahasuerus lose sleep? He could have had worrisome affairs of state. Or could it be that he was belatedly troubled by some guilt qualms over his collaboration in the plot to kill the Jews in his empire? Feelings of guilt can certainly contribute to sleeplessness. But perhaps the most reasonable assumption we can make is that he was the victim of plain, ordinary curiosity. Twice he had made the grand gesture, the offer almost anyone else would have jumped at, and twice his queen had left him dangling. A man, especially a husband, can stand just so much of that kind of thing. So, it is realistic to suppose he was consumed with curiosity as to what the morrow would bring. Mulling this over, with never a hint of a solution, could have kept his mind too alert for sleep. (I know a person who called a physician friend and said, "Could you please prescribe something for me? I go to bed but my head doesn't turn off, so I'm losing sleep.")

If we pondered till our heads became dizzy, we still would not know why the king could not sleep on that particular night. But the Bible makes one thing clear, and here perhaps is the real clue to the king's bout with insomnia: "Just as water is turned into irrigation ditches, so the Lord directs the king's thoughts" (Proverbs 21:1, TLB).

Should not this fact cause us to pay attention to the exhortation of 1 Timothy 2:1-3, with its plea that we pray for kings?

So the book was brought as requested. "The Life and Times of Xerxes" the chronicle may have been titled, and we can imagine this Eastern monarch bolstered up in his ornate bed, stroking his beard in gleeful recollection as the tale was retold—in this land of storytellers.

Victories in battle—captive slaves to add to his realm—wealth—the spoils of war—personal triumphs—and then—

"Stop! Read that again—slowly," the king commands.

Ah! A plot against his own life. Of course! A forgotten incident. Forgotten—but recorded against such a time as this (2:21-23). Now he recalls the whole affair.

The court reader would have continued with the record, but the king's interest was aroused. All thought of sleep left him; his mind aroused to action. And it is to his everlasting credit that this emperor was not at that moment callously mindful only of his own narrow escape. His mind went to his rescuer.

"How was this man Mordecai—he who saved my life—rewarded?" was the king's question. "What was done for him to show the king's gratitude? How was he honored? A king must never be under obligation to a captive. Read. What says the chronicle? What honor and dignity has been done to this man?"

"Nothing, sire. There is nothing done for him." The answer was simple because the record was blank. Nothing had been done by way of rewarding the man who had saved the king's life.

It took a sleepless night and a king's whim to have a scroll read to him, to have the story brought into focus. What if it had been a night or so later that the king could not sleep?

So do men, from peasants to kings on their thrones, serve the purpose of God and further His plan for His own.

Stirred now to action, the king wasted no time. "Who is around the court at this time?" he asked, a scheme already formulating in his mind.

And who but Haman is hanging around at such an hour! He too must have had little sleep, intent as he was on obtaining the king's consent to his own nefarious scheme. And here, a great principle comes into focus.

MAN PROPOSES—GOD DISPOSES

Haman could dream up his diabolical scheme. He could carry it so far. He could order that the gallows be erected. But apparently he could not, on his own, condemn a man to death. The king had the final word.

What a comfort it is to know that Satan can plan and plot, but he can go just so far and no farther with a child of God. Such is clearly taught in the book of Job (1:1—2:6). Satan could plague Job unmercifully, but he could not take his life. Likewise, man can plot evil, but God has the last word.

With the gallows silhouetted in the half light, it takes little imagination to visualize the next scene.

The vain, pompous Haman, thoroughly deluded by his grandiose opinion of himself, when welcomed by the king, is far too elated to notice the impersonal tone as the monarch poses the question: "What shall be done unto the man whom the king delighteth to honour?" (6:6).

The measure of Haman's inflated ego is in verse 6: "Now Haman thought in his heart, To whom would the king delight to do honour more than to myself?" And he was quick with his suggestions as to what that honor should be.

In detail he outlined what should be done for the man the king had in mind to honor. Make him "king for a day," he recommends. Dress him in the king's robes—crown and all—mount him on the king's own horse and give him a ticker-tape parade all along Main Street, with the heralds proclaiming the man's great deeds. (Did Haman have in mind, possibly, what the Pharaoh of Egypt had done for Joseph "whom he delighted to honor"—Genesis 41:42-43?)

We can almost hear the hiss of the air as it escapes from Haman's balloon: "Then the king said to Haman, Make haste, and take the apparel and the horse, as thou hast said, and do even so to Mordecai, the Jew, who sitteth at the king's gate. Let nothing fail of all that thou hast spoken" (6:10).

Mordecai the Jew! Was there no escaping the influence of this insignificant man! Who could measure the indignity, the humiliation in the black heart and mind of Haman in that moment? Did his eyes travel in the direction of the high gallows in the courtyard? "Mordecai's turn would come," he must have consoled himself.

"Let nothing fail of all that thou hast spoken," the king cautions. The irony of fate. Can you picture it? How well the poet James Russell Lowell wrote:

> Truth forever on the scaffold,
> Wrong forever on the throne,—
> Yet that scaffold sways the future,
> And, behind the dim unknown,
> Standeth God within the shadow,
> Keeping watch above his own.

Never was this more graphically demonstrated than in the life of Mordecai! In the very shadow of the scaffold that was to have spelled death for him, he is honored, and the one whose evil intent it was to kill him is, instead, delegated to bestow the honor.

Poetic justice? More than that, it is the providence of God. Who can dispute that man proposes, but God disposes!

Sometimes, through no fault of our own, and indeed when we may be trying to help someone else, or to serve the Lord as we understand He is leading us, we find ourselves in a dire strait. It is at such times that we see the hand of God intervening. His Word has clearly said, "No weapon that is formed against thee shall prosper" (Isaiah 54:17a). Also, there is blessed solace in the words of Paul, who knew so much about being persecuted and misunderstood in his service for Christ, "Let us not be weary in well doing, for in due season we shall reap" (Galatians 6:9), and "Thanks be unto God, who always causeth us to triumph in Christ" (2 Corinthians 2:14)..

This was Mordecai's season to reap, and the weapon that was formed against him could not prosper. He was about to be the hero in a triumphal parade!

HOW ARE THE MIGHTY FALLEN

The parade over, Mordecai returns to the palace while his would-be executor skulks home like a dog licking his wounds. Gone the triumph with which he had shared his delight over the queen's invitation just a short time ago.

Again he shares his experiences with his wife and his friends. Where did Zeresh, Haman's wife, get the wisdom with which she seeks to advise her husband? Like the wife of Pontius Pilate, Haman's wife speaks possibly better than she knows: prophetic truth.

"If Mordecai be of the seed of the Jews, before whom thou hast begun to fall, thou shalt not prevail against him, but shalt surely fall before him" (6:13).

She speaks wisdom indeed, as history has borne out. At that point Haman would have been well advised to take a step back and view as objectively as possible his next move. In the ears of a less arrogant man, the words "Thou shalt not prevail against him" might have rung, causing thoughtful reevaluation of his own position and planning.

"While they were yet talking with him" leads us to infer that

Haman was giving his wife and his well-meaning friends an argument.

And in the meantime, Esther's party plans are going ahead. Perhaps Haman perked up as he was hastily summoned to Esther's banquet. Did he think, *I may yet get a chance to revenge myself on Mordecai?*

After a sleepless night and a morning that saw him pay his debt of gratitude to Mordecai, the king also makes his way to Esther's quarters.

What are her thoughts, her fears? Has she too spent a sleepless night?

One thing we can be certain of: Mordecai was not far away as the hour for the banquet drew near.

Was he meditating on the providence of God that had brought about this incredible day? Was he pondering as to what next awaited him? Would Haman's evil scheme yet be fulfilled? Or was another joyful turn of events about to transpire? What was personal honor when his whole race is still condemned to death?

From our vantage point of history, we can reflect on how the mighty are fallen. More importantly, we are dramatically reminded that God made a covenant with the Jews as a people, and that frequently covenant-keeping has extended to the individual Jew.

Unquestionably, the last place Haman wanted to go at that time was to a party—any party—but God's plan called for Haman's appearance at Esther's banquet. We will meet him there.

To Think About and Do

1. What are your thoughts regarding such a normal happening as a sleep problem being the key factor in furthering God's plan for His people's deliverance?
2. How do you identify with the problem of occasional sleeplessness? What is your personal prescription at such times?

3. What part did the keeping of precise records play in the outcome of the insomnia incident? (What if God had not given us His precise written record? How would we know for sure that Jesus intervened to save us from eternal death?)

4. How vital was the *timing* in the sequence of events in this chapter? Can you think of occasions when the Lord has done something for you "in the nick of time"? Or, perhaps you have chafed at God's "delay," only to find out later that His timing was perfect. What can you learn at such times?

5. What commendable characteristic did the king display? Were you prepared for what this glimpse into his character reveals?

    If you are sometimes concerned about appreciation and gratitude apparently going out of style, what little and big steps are you taking day by day to restore such virtues in everyday contacts with people?

6. A byplay is going on at the same time the king could not sleep? What was it, and how did it help the king to speedily implement his good intentions toward his deliverer?

    What is the importance of activating a good impulse immediately, if possible? Share with the group something that has happened to you because you stopped what you were doing to carry out a good idea to help someone. Perhaps the Lord brought to mind someone's special need for prayer, or an encouraging phone call, or a letter. Perhaps it was practical help you were nudged by the Holy Spirit to give where it was needed. Or perhaps there was a time when you realized God was speaking to you about one of the ways you could help, but you pushed it to the back of your mind for "when I have time"—and the opportunity to be a blessing was lost.

7. What does the divine principle that *God* has the last word in our affairs say to you? As you believe this and medi-

tate on it, how will this change your attitude toward what comes your way?

8. Why, in your opinion, does God sometimes not intervene until the gallows is erected?

8

Marked for Immortality

I and my people . . . are doomed to destruction and slaughter. If we were only to be sold as slaves, perhaps I could remain quiet (7:4, TLB).

Read Esther 7:1-10

The day had started strangely—this day of destiny for a whole race of people.

Where the king's decree had already been delivered by the swift-riding posts in areas of his empire, black despair must have gripped the people. We can imagine a family scene as the tidings sink into their amazed consciousness.

The aged grandfather can take no comfort in the knowledge that although life for him is nearing an end, the child playing at his knee will carry on the ancient, unique tradition that had kept his race distinctive.

"Young and old—little children and women," the king had decreed.

Neither could this elderly Jew console himself with the thought that in some distant province the Jews would survive, and that their little children would be safe to play.

"All the Jews," the grim document stated.

And the fateful thirteenth of Adar hastened on.

How could they know—these Jews who lived in the far-flung provinces—that their fate lay in the hands of a woman? A woman who even then awaited her opportunity to plead their cause.

Had they known, perhaps they would have called to mind another point in history when God had chosen a young girl to play a major role in their nation's deliverance—Miriam, who watched by the riverbank as God set the stage for the drama of Moses, the emancipator.

DISCLOSURE

It was a different Haman from the strutting autocrat of chapter 5 who accompanied the king to Esther's chambers in the palace. There is a distinct inference that he had delayed until the king sent messengers to bring him (see 6:14). Had he heeded his wife's prophetic words? Were they strumming in his brain? Apparently something had happened to change her mind, since she encouraged Haman to get rid of Mordecai.

"If Mordecai be of the seed of the Jews . . . thou shalt not prevail . . . thou shalt surely fall before him," she now asserted.

Meanwhile has the king perhaps begun to connect his queen's hesitant request with Haman? Has something leaked to him, apart from the incident with Mordecai?

Again we see the king's gracious treatment of Esther. It is beginning to sound like a record when the needle sticks! "What is thy petition? . . . What is thy request? and it shall be performed, even to the half of the kingdom" (7:2).

As the words must surely have echoed in her brain since first she heard them, so Esther hears them again.

Did the contrasting possibilities race through her mind: "half of the kingdom" or, depending on the king's reaction to her request, the loss of not only her crown, but also her head!

But some five days before, Esther had determined which turn she would take when she arrived at this crossroad. Her resolute, "If I perish, I *perish*" marked the course she would take—the crucial decision that has given her a place in history.

"What is thy petition, Queen Esther?" What is your request? She could delay no longer. She had both petition and request ready to present.

For we are sold, I and my people, to be destroyed, to be slain, and to perish. But if we had been sold for bondmen and bondwomen, I had held my tongue, although the enemy could not [compensate] for the king's damage (7:4).

She pleads for her life. This was her petition. And how wise the order in which she made both petition and request. For, her own life in jeopardy, how could she intercede for her people?

It is questionable that the king heard all that she said. His queen, pleading for her life! This, then, was the reason she dared approach him unbidden. This the request for which she had felt the need to prepare him by banqueting and wine! Hear her passionate plea for the doomed Jews. "We are sold, I and my people, to be destroyed, to be slain, and to perish." When our country is jeopardized, most of us are patriots.

If the king did a double-take at Esther's identifying herself as "of the people of the Jews," he gave no indication of it, for no doubt he was still aroused at the thought that her life was in danger.

THE TABLES ARE TURNED

The king hears her out, then answers by asking two questions that must have caused Haman to turn pale with terror.

"Who is he?" "Where is he?" and the inference of the second question is "that I might get my hands on him."

And in his indictment of the unknown offender, the king goes right to the core of all evil intent: "[Who] presumes in his heart to do so?" (see Mark 7:21).

Was chilling drama ever expressed in so few words?

Esther identifies the man as "that wicked Haman."

"Then Haman was afraid." Well might he be! Too well did he know that this was no time when a long, drawn-out court case might conceivably end in his acquittal. Swift justice would not tolerate delay.

In the heat of his anger, the king strode out into the palace garden. Did he by chance see the gallows high in the garden of Haman's property?

More than blind rage must have motivated the king as he stalked out of the banquet area to walk in the palace garden. What conflicting emotions were riding high, causing him to seek solitude, as others have done before and since, in order to sort out their feelings! Amazement that his queen was a victim of the plot against the Jews? That she herself was a Jewess? Chagrin that he, himself, had been such a fool as to not see Haman for what he was; for elevating this man to such a high rank; for letting Haman manipulate him into agreeing to his evil scheme; that his confidence in Haman had been so misplaced? Kings especially must like to think of themselves as having good judgment in such matters.

Transcending all other emotions, the king must surely have had feelings of personal guilt. For while Haman has instigated the plot and had drawn the king into it as a collaborator, Haman could not have carried it out. The king's seal provided the authority that would see the evil scheme was implemented.

Queen Esther showed grace in her denunciation and exposure of Haman. She could have said, as Nathan the prophet had said to David the king, "Thou art the man!" (2 Samuel 12:7). She did not. But this did not relieve Ahasuerus of responsibility for his part. His own heart must have condemned him, and guilt is hard to live with.

He reenters the banquet room, his thoughts unwritten. We will never know whether at that moment he was blaming himself as much as Haman.

The wheel of fate has spun 180 degrees. Proud Haman! When first we met him, he was disconcerted because Mordecai refused to bow to him; now he begs and pleads for his very life, before the foster daughter of Mordecai.

First Haman stands and pleads his case before the queen, who is lounging, as was the custom, in banqueting in those days. Then, desperate, he throws himself to the floor by her couch.

But—one look at the scene of Haman on his knees before the queen's couch, and all reason leaves the king. His thinking must have been that a man who had been so conniving, who had inveigled him into a dastardly plot, would stop at nothing. So it is today. He who is found guilty of one crime, is readily suspect of other greater crimes.

Uncontrolled rage now governed the king. And Haman, who had mercilessly given the Jews no chance to present their case, was now confronted with the same justice.

His wife's prophetic words were coming true. How black and terrible the king's anger must have been. To the servants standing by, it had but one significance: doom for Haman. In an act that has only one meaning even in our own day, the face of the condemned man was covered.

Into the drama again comes the chamberlain Harbonah. It had been his lot to be sent, with six other notables in the king's court, to bring Queen Vashti to the king's feast (1:10). He undoubtedly had lived through the dread fate of Vashti, had wondered who her successor would be, and had witnessed the rise of the young Esther to the throne.

GIVE A MAN ENOUGH ROPE

Had this man Harbonah and his fellow courtiers suffered at the hands of the pompous Haman? Had they secretly deplored his animosity toward the Jews in general and toward Mordecai in particular?

Certain it is that this man made no effort to appeal to the king for either time or clemency for Haman. As though suggesting the ease with which a stage set might be arranged, he advises the king that the means of executing Haman is right at hand—in the condemned man's own back yard. All was in readiness for use.

And note the details. It could not have mattered to the king the height of the gallows. But he was told anyway (7:9). The more significant information—"the gallows . . . which Haman had made for Mordecai"—would lead one to believe that Harbonah got some personal satisfaction out of relaying this item of news.

By this time, we can imagine the king was more than a little confused. Haman plotting to hang Mordecai!

Scheming Haman never got his opportunity to ask the king's approval of that particular plot, even though he had made a point of being early at the palace. The king's inability to sleep and the consequent uncovering of the assassination plot that Mordecai had foiled: all this had worked against the schemer.

Another detail Harbonah had not left out: "Mordecai, who had spoken good for the king."

The story was fresh in Ahasuerus' mind. He needed no prompting. Here was a man who had saved his own life. It was not enough that Mordecai had been feted and honored. He must now be avenged. And the case against Haman was compounded.

No judge. No jury. No long hours of presenting evidence. Not finding that the accused was a victim of circumstances or that his early environment explained his behavior and consequently exonerated him. Nothing like that. In the way in which the king had turned to a ready source to arrange to reward Mordecai, so he availed himself of his chamberlain's information and suggestion.

> And Harbonah, one of the chamberlains, said before the king, Behold also, the gallows fifty cubits high, which Haman had made for Mordecai, who hath spoken good for the king, standeth in the house of Haman. Then the king said, Hang him thereon (7:9).

Just like that!

"So they hanged Haman on the gallows he had prepared for Mordecai. Then was the king's wrath pacified" (7:10).

But Esther's problem was by no means wholly solved. Her petition had been granted. Her own life was secure in the king's hands. But what of her request for her people? The king had not yet indicated what action he would take. What *could* he do, Esther might well have pondered. The messengers of doom were speeding throughout the empire, bearing the decree of the Medes and Persians which altereth not.

Haman, in his death, seems to have been "Unwept, unhonored, and unsung," while Esther is well on her way toward immortality.

To Think About and Do

1. We can never tell, by the way a day begins, how it will end. What important incident in your own experience bears out this truth?
2. What other women besides Esther, have been chosen for a vital role in Jewish history?
3. What is the significance for every generation in the warning given to Haman by his wife? Discuss the ways in which you can "bless" or "curse" Jewish people and thus bring God's blessing or displeasure upon your own life (see Genesis 12:2-3; Matthew 7:12; Galatians 6:7)?
4. In expressing her petition, how did Esther indicate that she placed herself in the same predicament as her people, even though she was the queen?
5. This might be a good time to pause and evaluate yourself as a loyal citizen of your country, and as a professed Christian.
6. In the light of the king's question, "Who presumes in his heart to do so?" consider the words of Jesus, Mark 7:21. Also see Proverbs 23:7a, and Philippians 4:8.
7. What emotions must have been churning within him as the king left Esther and Haman, to walk in the garden?
8. What timeless lesson can we learn from the king's denunciation of Haman when he saw Haman kneeling by the queen's couch?
9. In how many specific ways did Haman's plot to kill Mordecai boomerang? What should this teach us?

9

Crime in True Focus

He has been hanged upon the gallows because he
tried to destroy you (8:7, TLB).

Read Esther 8:1-8

We left the king well satisfied that justice had been meted
out. Not a moment's delay was permitted in which some
case might have been made for Haman. No long, drawn-out
legislation such as bogs down court procedures in our day.
Whatever we think of such haste when a life was at stake, we
have to keep in mind that Ahasuerus was a supreme monarch.
His disposition of the case appeased his personal wrath. "Then
was the king's wrath pacified" (7:10).

We can be sure that he was not the only one who was pleased
at the swift demise of Haman.

It is worthy of note that Haman is clearly designated "the
Jews' enemy." This, then, was his real crime—the crime for
which, ultimately, he paid with his life. How truly the Scriptures speak. "I will bless him that blesseth thee and curse him
that curseth thee" (Gen 12:3).

Hitler's heinous crime was unmitigated hatred against the
Jews—and the world will never forget. Part of the twenty-fifth
anniversary ceremonies in Israel in May 1973 consisted of
commemoration of the exterminating of six million Jews. When
some criticized Golda Meier for such remembrance, she stated,
"You who did not come to our aid shall not dictate to us now."

But for Esther and Mordecai, the king's sense of well-being

73

could spell ruin. Having rid himself of Haman, he could easily be caught up in the affairs of state of his vast empire. Again, thirty days could elapse before he would call for Esther, as had happened before. And, for the Jews, the ominous date with death drew ever closer.

In all of this, there is not one hint that Esther or Mordecai personally gloried in the death of Haman (even though Esther had called him "that wicked Haman"). It was not the man himself, but what he had initiated against their people that made him their enemy. This was no personal feud such as Haman had warred against Mordecai.

MEET MY FATHER

Esther had asked nothing of worldly goods for herself; no part of the kingdom of which she had been offered "up to the half." Nevertheless she was given Haman's estate. Possibly the king viewed his act as treason, and in such instances the criminal's possessions are normally forfeited to the state. The king undoubtedly was underlining his total outrage at Haman's daring to jeopardize the queen, by making over to her all that was Haman's.

A second benefit was that she was free to reveal her kinship to Mordecai. What a scene that must have been! Again we are reminded of Joseph (Genesis 45:3-4).

And how swiftly the drama was moving. All in one day was Mordecai marked for the gallows—in an about-face paraded as a hero—and now standing in the presence of the king in the role of an in-law: foster father to the queen. Not only so, but the king further honored him by entrusting to him the highest position next to his own (replay of Pharaoh and Joseph?).

In all the nearly four years that his foster daughter had walked in queenly robes, Mordecai had kept his and her secret. What strength of character and sense of mission did it take for him to refrain from confiding in a few friends in the palace; letting it be known that he was not in fact such a nobody. Never did he presume on the relationship, as a lesser spirit might have.

To the last detail was Mordecai vindicated.

BUT WHAT OF MY PEOPLE?

What was power? What was wealth and position, while the decree against the Jews was still in force? There had been no indication that the king had even heard Esther beyond her plea for her own life. Nothing of "We are sold, I and my people, to be destroyed, to be slain, and to perish."

Esther could wait no longer. No more banquets to set the climate for her request! She fell down at the king's feet and wept out her heartfelt plea.

As he had graciously done when first she had sought an audience with him, the king makes his royal gesture of extending his golden sceptre, symbol of authority, toward her.

Assured of a hearing, she now resorts to the ways of Easterners to this very day, and preludes her request with pleasing phrases. Then, from her lips comes one of the most poignant, heart-rending cries of the ages: "How can I endure to see the evil that shall come unto my people?"

The Berkeley version reads, "For how could I look on, while disaster strikes my people, and how, Oh, how, could I bear the ruin of my race!" (8:6).

Not merely *a* race—but my race, *my people*.

If only we might get a clear glimpse of this truth concerning eternal salvation. What of the final, ultimate end of our own people, unless they are saved in time? If we really believe in a heaven to gain and a hell to shun, we too would be on our knees before the only One who has the power to save. We would be evaluating our priorities, asking ourselves, of what worth is money, a new car, a fine position—any worldly gain— if we have to live with the knowledge that our own mother or dad, sister or brother, son or daughter is not saved? We would be crying out to God, "I *can't stand* it, Lord. Somehow, use me to reach them for You before it is too late."

While our people live, it is not too late.

"He that believeth not is condemned already," (John 3:18), Christ came into the world to *save sinners*. The decree against everyone of us was death, but one greater than Esther's kingly husband wrote a new decree. "For the law of the Spirit of life in Christ Jesus hath made me free from the law of sin and death" (Romans 8:2).

SOME THINGS EVEN A KING CANNOT DO

In her distress Esther seemingly had overlooked the fact that even the king could not countermand the decree—that he could not accede to her request that he "reverse the letters devised by Haman . . . to destroy all the Jews which are in all the king's provinces." There was that in the constitution of the Persian government which forbade the reversal of a decree sealed with the king's ring. So rigid was this code that to this day it is proverbial: the law of the Medes and the Persians altereth not.

Not at this time does Esther reiterate what she had said earlier (7:4b): "If we had been sold [I and my people] for bondmen and bondwomen, I had held my tongue." And then— another aspect of the situation—she had called to the king's attention that the Jews were an *asset* and that the enemy who would destroy them was doing damage to the empire. (In this connection, consider what the situation must have been in Egypt the morning after the departure of the Hebrew slaves. How many building projects must have ground to a halt with the loss of the brickmakers!)

The inference is that Esther gladly would have joined her Jewish brethren in slavery, if that had to be. The Jews had survived captivity before, and they would again. It was their *lives* she was pleading for. Perhaps when confronted by extremity, we are all patriots; we want to identify with our own people. Esther had no wish for personal immunity, as evidenced by her "How can I endure to see the destruction of my people?"

We cannot know whether the king's love for Esther or his reactivated rage against Haman motivated him. But, decisive as ever, he now shows himself equally resourceful.

IT IS UP TO YOU TWO NOW

Turning to Esther and to "Mordecai the Jew," he offered his solution to the seemingly impossible situation.

> Look! I have handed Haman's belongings over to Esther, and him have they hanged on gallows; because he would lay hands on the Jews [note his emphasis on this last phrase]. Now you yourselves write for the Jews as you think best, in the king's name and seal it with the royal signet ring; for a document that is written in the king's name is sealed with the royal signet ring no one may reverse (8:7-8, Berkeley).

It is hard to believe we are hearing the same man who willingly gave his accord to the death-decreeing letters, then sat down to drink with the perpetrator, Haman! Does this say to us that the number one man in any country is no better than those whose counsel he listens to?

What a moment that must have been for Queen Esther and her foster father, Mordecai. All the despair, all the fears, all the self-sacrifice that enabled Esther to say, "If I perish, I perish" and brave the wrath of the king; all the fasting, sackcloth, tears, and uncertainty—it was all over. Or was it?

Certainly the king was now on the side of the Jews. But was it even now too late? More than two months had elapsed since Haman put his evil intent into motion.

Can you picture what must have happened, what we can read between the lines of sparse detail given? Surely there never was a more critical huddle as to the next maneuver!

"Write ye for the Jews," the king had recommended. Did he feel his own inadequacy to direct what should be best written? He keeps using the word *Jews* as if it were new to him and important, but out of his own realm (literally).

What would you have written or advised Mordecai to have

written by the scribes? It would take a Solomon to make such a life and death decision.

And still we do not read that they prayed (unlike Nehemiah who prayed to the God of heaven and spoke to the king, Nehemiah 2:4-5).

Nevertheless, the hand of the Lord was upon the Jews and upon the queen and Prime Minister Mordecai in Shushan, the palace.

The record might well read, "That night the king, the queen, and Mordecai *did* sleep." They had had a busy day.

To Think About and Do

1. What are your thoughts concerning the swiftness of Ahasuerus' justice? (Keep in mind that Mordecai would have had no trial. If Haman had his way, this would have been Mordecai's execution day.)
2. With what New Testament concept does retaliation conflict? (see Romans 12:19).
3. The Bible goes to the heart of the matter in indicting and condemning Haman. He was the Jews' enemy. What should this say to us as God's people when unbelievers would persecute us?
4. What does this chapter teach concerning the rewards that come to those who seek others' welfare above their own?
5. Read Esther 8:6 slowly, carefully, and thoughtfully. Then read it again in the context of today and your own family and relatives. Considering it in the light of the possible near return of Christ, can you endure it that some of your loved ones are not ready to meet Him?
6. Esther knew what could not be done, but she did not let it deter her from pleading with the king. Are you sometimes guilty of allowing the impossibles to engross you to the exclusion of working through to a possible solution?
7. In every situation that concerned him, we have seen this pagan king as a man of decisive action. In what ways

could you better serve the Lord by being decisive; by taking action when this is called for? List some specific ways and be alert for opportunities.

This chapter points out that evil can be reversed—when even one key person is sufficiently concerned and aroused. Think of that!

10

Special Delivery

Mordecai wrote in the name of King Ahasuerus . . .
and sent the letters by swift carriers (8:10, TLB).

Read Esther 8:9-17

We left Esther and Mordecai with the king's blessing on their efforts to undo the evil Haman had plotted and initiated. The situation calls for action swift and certain.

SUMMON THE SCRIBES

Again the royal scribes and translators were summoned and given a colossal task. From the highest offices down to the petty officials in each of the 127 provinces, all were on the mailing list: princes, governors, deputies; each had to be addressed in his own language and dialect. This was not a matter of minor differences in language. The territory to be covered was—incredibly—"from India to Ethiopia," with all the variety of languages concerned. The palace of Shushan must have boasted an impressive staff of linguists! The Jews, also, in each part of the empire were notified.

We are not told how long the letter-writing campaign took, just that the scribes were called to the palace two months and ten days later than their summons by Haman. Finally, the last letter was written and sealed with the king's signet ring; the mail bags were filled.

SADDLE THE HORSES

On came the posts atop the nation's speediest horses and mules, the royal steeds bred for the king's service.

Suddenly, nothing was too good for the Jews. Nothing was to be spared that would aid their cause.

Important as was the king's seal and the speed of the riders, equally crucial was the content of the letters. How simple it would have been if Mordecai had been able to just write "Cancel the decree of the thirteenth of Adar" and have thousands of copies zeroxed. But such was not the case in that day of handwritten everything. Brevity was necessary if the letters would be written and speeded on their way, yet the message must be indisputably clear to every person concerned.

Never was a document more legally binding on those to whom it was sent.

What did it say? How would the Jews be delivered?

THE REPRIEVE

> Wherein the king granted the Jews who were in every city to gather themselves together, and to stand for their life, to destroy, to slay, and to cause to perish, all the power of the people and province that would assault them, both little ones and women, and to take the spoil of them for prey, upon one day in all the provinces of king Ahasuerus, namely, upon the thirteenth day of the twelfth month, which is the month Adar (8:11-12).

If you recall the text of Haman's edict, you will note the close similarity of the counterdecree.

The Jews throughout the Medo-Persian Empire would not be powerless, not be defenseless when the thirteenth arrived. Rather, with the sanction—in fact with a cheering section of officials who must have been confused, to say the least, when edict number two reached them—the Jews would defend themselves, their families, and their property.

Significantly, again "no weapon formed against them would prosper:" it was a foregone conclusion—can we put it more strongly and say it was predestined—that the Jews would be victorious.

We need only recall a certain six days in the sixth month,

the month Sivan in the Hebrew calendar, of the year nineteen hundred and sixty-seven, to be persuaded that the Jewish people are abundantly, demonstrably able to emerge victorious in battle.

As Haman the Jew-hater was hanged on the gallows he had prepared for Mordecai the Jew, so now the plot he had instigated had boomeranged. If only the letters arrive in time! Speed the horses. Hurry, hurry! Haman's letters have a big headstart: possibly three months.

NOT VENGEANCE; SELF DEFENSE

The plan did not call for guerilla warfare, or a long, drawn-out series of attack and counterattack. It was to be a strategic, decisive, one day, all-out battle for their lives. The one proviso being that it was directed at "all the power of the province and the people that would assault them" (8:11). The day decreed for the Jews' defense was the day already decreed for their slaughter; their genocide. They were not the aggressors; they were to *defend* themselves against those who were prepared to annihilate them.

We need to keep in mind that God was not dealing with individual Jews; He was keeping a covenant with the race of people He had chosen.

Can we again take a glimpse into a home where the blighting decree had cast its pall: the inhabitants awaiting as though on death row, the approach of the thirteenth day of the twelfth month.

Suddenly a shout goes up as the riders on foaming steeds deliver their written reprieve. Almost unbelieving, with trembling hands the official takes a copy of the letter. Light breaks like a summer morning as the truth dawns on him. He hurries to his home.

Not like the animals for slaughter would his family be led to their death. They would fight for their lives!

New, fresh, vigorous blood begins to course through the veins of young and old alike. They were *not* marked for death.

A chance for life was offered to them—and the preparations for defense were begun.

So it must have been as from town to town, province to province the message was carried. Did ever missionaries carry a more joyous message? What a privilege was theirs to be the bearers of glad tidings!

The resilient Jews quickly bounce from despair to hope.

THERE IS JOY IN SHUSHAN

As for Mordecai, that day when the decree went forth, he stepped from Shushan the palace, his sackcloth replaced by royal garb: blue, white, and purple, with a crown of gold where ashes had been. God had literally given him the garments of praise for the spirit of heaviness and the oil of joy for mourning (Isaiah 61:3).

Most fittingly, the mandate was first announced to the inhabitants of Shushan. Indeed it would have been impossible to keep it from them with all the comings and goings at the palace. We recall that at Haman's decree they had been perplexed. At the new turn of events "the city of Shushan rejoiced and was glad" (8:15). This speaks volumes for the contribution the Jews made in Shushan and the relationships they enjoyed with their neighbors.

What of the Jews themselves in Shushan? We can believe that the mothers directed that every available candle be brought and lit. Light is always a big part of Jewish celebrating, and we read (8:16) "the Jews had light."

Had the announcement been officially made that the *queen* was Jewish? I wonder.

From her departure from Mordecai's home to be among the candidates for queen, her own people must have known who had replaced Vashti.

They had gladness and joy, these warmhearted, emotional, patriotic people. We can fancy they danced on the streets for joy.

They had honor. They were being treated like human beings, not slave chattels. Without honor, how could they have known light, or gladness, or joy?

The spiritual analogy is plain. When we come to Christ and accept Him as Saviour, the spiritual death decree is revoked. We do not have to do battle, for Jesus conquered sin and death for us. Now, in Him, we can sing, "I have light in my soul for which long I had sought," and "Jesus comes with joy and gladness."

As for honor, we are honored to be the children of God; heirs of God and joint heirs with Jesus Christ. We are a chosen generation, a royal priesthood. What more honor can we ask?

For the Jews of that day, it was one long celebration, rolling along from place to place until in all the provinces there was a feast and a good day (8:17).

Oh, they were not out of the woods yet. But they had been "released from the snare of the fowler."

And because smart people all over the world know a good thing when they see it and usually want to get in on it, many a non-Jewish person, caught up in all the light and gladness, decided "this is for me" and converted—they became Jews.

Did they, with the insight and foresight of Haman's wife, sense that there was a special providence taking care of these Jewish people, and that it was the better part of discretion to be on their side? Or, were they, perhaps, expressing a universal need to know such a God?

In our own day, a parallel situation is not unknown. For example, during the desperate days preceding the birth of the nation of Bangladesh, many Hindus sought out Christian missionaries with the plea for a paper stating that they were Christians. For some, this was "life insurance" for in the eyes of the West Pakistan military, it was a crime to be a Hindu, and the punishment was death. Because "Christian" was being equated with "Western," these Hindus sought the protection that being a Christian would afford. For others, however, it was a time of decision following long months of missionary endeavor.

They were worthy of the paper for they had committed their lives to Christ.

There is, in the action of the Medes and Persians of Ahasuerus' empire, a foretaste of Zechariah 8:23. "Thus says the LORD of hosts: In those days ten men from nations of varied languages shall take hold of a Jew's coat, hold on to it and say, "Let us go with you, for we have heard that God is with you" (Berkeley).

What better thing can God's people be known for?

And Queen Esther—where is she, and what is she doing during these days? Did she perhaps call for another three days of fasting and thanksgiving? Was she busy making sure that, when the crucial thirteenth of Adar arrived, her people would be suitably equipped for battle? The record is silent. We can, however, believe that she was pondering the ways of God that would take her, an obscure captive, and place her on the throne beside the great emperor "for such a time as this."

To Think About and Do

1. Think of how much of the epic of Esther hinges on letter writing. Consider the alternatives available to us today, then relate this to how slow communication aided the Jews in that day.

2. What does the content of the letter do to you? Perhaps you would have preferred that God send a destroying angel rather than that the solution to the Jews' problem be a bloody war?

3. In what sense can the "posts" be likened to missionaries of the gospel?

4. What instances in your own life demonstrate the exchange of "garments of praise for the spirit of heaviness"? Share the blessing so that someone else will be encouraged.

5. Discuss with others the spiritual analogy of "light, and gladness, and joy, and honour" (v. 16).

6. Ask yourself what attitudes and actions and expressed beliefs of mine would cause someone to want to join me and

become a Christian? If your self-evaluation leaves you dissatisfied, talk to God about this. He wants to help you to be the best possible witness for Him, and He wants you to be happy in your Christian life; not dissatisfied.

11

Fight for Your Life

The day the Jews' enemies had hoped to vanquish them . . . the Jews gathered . . . throughout the king's provinces to defend themselves (9:1-2, TLB).

Read Esther 9:1-18

Discussing the book of Esther with a writer who is not a Christian but who appreciates the drama in its chapters, I was not too surprised when he said, "If I had been writing it, I think I would have opted for a different happy ending—one a bit less gory."

This may be a commendable suggestion except that the Bible deals primarily in realism, not idealism.

God's people in dire peril of their life. The only out for them was this opportunity given them to fight for their lives. And victory for one side can be had only through defeat for the other.

It goes without saying that the Jews had more to fight for. Theirs was a patriotic, a religious, a historic cause. Some of them were far from Jerusalem; it may be that many of them had never set foot on the land God had promised to His chosen people. But there is something in all of us, that when our heritage is threatened, we can forget lesser issues and unite in the greater cause. It is the "breathes there a man with soul so dead" of which the insightful Shakespeare writes. So the Jews united (9:2), and in unity is strength. At a less critical time, a number of differences may have divided the Jewish people, as indeed they do today.

As Christians, we would undoubtedly strengthen our position and present a more solid front to the non-Christian world if we would be willing sometimes to submerge external and often not scripturally based differences. Is this not what Jesus prayed for, in His prayer that we might be one (John 17:20-21)? Our credibility as Christ's followers appears to have been the issue. One of the popular songs of today is, "We are one in the Spirit; we are one in the Lord."

As for the enemy, they were merely carrying out orders to annihilate this people, on an edict signed by the emperor. In united action against their enemy, the Jews were battling for ethnic survival.

DIVINE PSYCHOLOGICAL WARFARE

There are some interesting factors in the record. We might see it as a form of psychological warfare. For one thing, a kind of legend was building around the Jews (reminiscent of Joshua 2:8-11 when Rahab told the two spies, "The inhabitants of the land melt in terror because of you," Berkeley).

We will never know what the tales were that were being told concerning the Jews and their "in" with Deity. But whether true or conjured up by terror, they had a powerful influence on the inhabitants of Ahasuerus' empire.

This is a subject that leaves room for much thought. We might ponder whether our Christian life is so dynamic that even people who avowedly do not share our faith, nevertheless are awed by their certainty that God is with us.

During the years that my son was a member of New York University track team, I rarely missed a meet. Naturally I became acquainted with the coach. Some years later he wrote, "I used to watch you. You had one eye on Bruce and the other on Someone else. Bruce couldn't lose." Be that as it may, somehow this veteran track coach recognized a power he did not have; a greater Power. Subsequent letters led me to believe that he may have sought the Lord for himself.

The influence of the Jews upon their enemies doubtless had little to do with any strength or prowess attributed to an individual Jew or to some group of Jews. They had no David to go against the "Goliath" of that day; no visible Elijah to call down fire on their enemies. No, it was not fear of the known but of the *unknown* that made defectors of the enemy. Apart from this factor, they may have been courageous and daring.

Honesty will make any of us admit to fear of the unknown, even though we are able to muster up courage to face the dangers we do know.

IF YOU CAN'T BEAT THEM, JOIN THEM

Another decisive factor in the Jews' favor was that they had officialdom on their side. The high military, the top administrators, the representatives of the king all supported the Jews in their battle. We are not told how they supported them, but it is reasonable to assume that they made weapons of war available and possibly arranged for training. Also, themselves seized with dread, they may have communicated fear to thousands of people, who, convinced they could not beat the Jews, decided to join them.

Add to this the aura of greatness that was beginning to surround the name of Mordecai. News of his elevation to the second place in the empire must have made the populace think twice about killing the Jews. You will recall that Mordecai had never made a secret of being a Jew. And we now read that "this man Mordecai grew steadily more powerful" (9:3, Berkeley).

Who would have thought, just a few chapters back, that we would hear Mordecai called "great" and even "greater"? "When a man's ways please the LORD, he maketh even his enemies to be at peace with him" (Proverbs 16:7).

In Shushan, the king was warming up to the whole project he had helped initiate. It may have been meat and drink to a war-loving monarch. He certainly seems to have taken a lively interest in the casualty list. (If this appears callous, ask yourself, How did I react to the day after day score of the American and North Vietnamese casualties of war?)

An eye for an eye

If the whole thing seems wantonly bloody, perhaps we need to consider the fact that in any generation, men have warring hearts. The history of wars is pretty much the story of human nature. Then, too, the Jews, unlike the enemy, did not plan wholesale slaughter. Their intent was solely to defend themselves against those who rose up against them.

Moreover, this was the era of an eye for an eye and a tooth for a tooth. Not yet had the greater Lawgiver come; not yet had the new commandment been given to love your enemies.

Sometimes we have New Testament expectations of Old Testament persons and situations. Frequently, in the same frame of reference, we have Christian expectations of those who are not believers.

Then too, as Christians, sometimes we tend to idealize the Jew, in the context that Jews are somehow special. They are— as a people. And God's covenant is with them as a people, not as individuals. As individuals, Jews are just like we are. They are not all Moses or Joshua or David or Esther. It gives balance to our thinking when we keep in mind that while God does choose out and use certain Jews to carry forward His plan of the ages, at the same time millions of Jews all over the world live everyday pretty much like their Gentile neighbors. They are religious, and they are irreligious. They are sinners as are all men until they accept God's offer of salvation through Christ's atonement.

When a Jew *is* God-fearing, generally his zeal knows no bounds. Many such have lived for the day that Israel would be their national home. I recall a sight so moving that although I observed it in 1951, it is still vivid in my mind. The scene was New York harbor.

In one of the piers was a ship flying the flag of Israel, with its Star of David. Alongside the ship milled a throng of Jewish people, the Orthodox men and boys easily distinguishable by their garb and side curls. The older men, among them rabbis, wept openly, and the tears spilled over and ran down their beards. They were seeing with their own eyes the first ship of the Israeli fleet, a Corvette purchased from the Canadian government. They were seeing more, much more. They were seeing the fulfillment of prophecy, Israel taking her place among the nations. From what I could observe, the older men were solemnly impressing the meaning of that hour on the younger men and boys.

As I write this, Israel is celebrating the twenty-fifth anniversary of her national independence, and it is more than an anniversary; it is the realization of a centuries-old dream of rebuilding an historic homeland.

Something of this spirit must have activated the Jews in the empire of the Medes and Persians.

His attention focused on the Jews and their progress in the fight for survival, the king again turned to the concerns of his queen.

"What else can I do for you, Queen Esther?" he asks. It is worth noting that this time there is no offer of up to half of his kingdom. Perhaps he had learned that other than material possessions engrossed his queen.

> And the king said unto Esther the queen, The Jews have slain and destroyed five hundred men in Shushan the palace, and the ten sons of Haman; what have they done in the rest of the king's provinces? now what is thy petition? and it shall be granted thee: or what is thy request further? and it shall be done. Then said Esther, If it please the king, let it be granted to the Jews which are in Shushan to do to morrow also according unto this day's decree, and let Haman's ten sons be hanged upon the gallows. And the king commanded it so to be done: and the decree was given at Shushan; and they hanged Haman's ten sons. For the Jews that were in Shushan gathered themselves together on the fourteenth day

also of the month Adar, and slew three hundred men at Shushan; but on the prey they laid not their hand (9:12-15).

We might be shocked by the request Esther made at this time, but she had done her history homework. Was she recalling an edict given to King Saul, and what happened because of his disobedience? Saul had been commanded to slay the Amalekites, including their king, Agag. But Saul chose to keep the king alive. The unhappy story is recorded in 1 Samuel.

> Samuel said to Saul. . . . The Lord of hosts says: I have in mind what Amalek did to Israel. . . . Now, then, you go and strike down Amalek; destroy all he has; spare none. . . . Saul struck down Amalek. . . . However, Saul and the people spared Agag [the Amalekite king] (1 Samuel 15:1-9, Berkeley).

According to many Bible students, Haman was a descendant of Agag.

Haman was dead. No more would he wreak his vengeance on the Jews. But Esther may have been thinking of the generations yet to come and protecting them from the offspring of Haman who might have, if allowed to live, perpetuated what their father had begun.

We should note that, unlike Saul who took the spoil, the Jews in Esther's time did not (9:10). They wiped out the enemy but scorned to take the spoils of war.

So, out in the provinces, the thirteenth dawned, that "day that the enemies of the Jews hoped to have power over them" (9:1). But "the Jews gathered themselves together . . . and no man could withstand them" (9:2).

A Hitler, a Nasser, and others would arise. But for the present, the thirteenth of Adar was robbed of its black dread.

One would have to live through such an experience in order to fully enter into the feelings of the Jewish people on that day. However, to the extent to which we can identify with them, we can rejoice with them in their feasting and frolicking.

And more letters were about to be written. For here were two persons—Esther and Mordecai—who had reason to respect the power of the pen.

To Think About and Do

1. With reference to the opinion expressed in the opening paragraph of this eleventh chapter, we can take heart knowing that the day is coming when men will learn war no more (see Isaiah 2:4; Micah 4:3).

2. As Christians "fighting the good fight of faith," we are not always united against our common foe. On what basis should we be united? Whose purposes are best served when we allow factions to divide us? We cannot make Christian unity, but the Bible instructs us to "[endeavor] to keep the unity of the Spirit" (Ephesians 4:3). Discuss how we can try to do this. Also read Psalm 133:1 in this connection.

3. What made the Jews' cause morally right?

4. In your opinion, why did the king not repeat his "up to the half of my kingdom" offer?

5. Esther has not appeared to be a vengeful person. Yet here she is making a shocking request. What makes this understandable? Can you think of a time when you shrank from some drastic move, yet you knew it was the only thing to do in the circumstance? In retrospect, would you do the same thing in a similar situation?

6. The Jews engaged in a war that was strictly for self defense. But they were no looters, even though permission had been given for them to take the spoil (8:11). Who would benefit when the fighting was all over? Those who had chosen not to rise up against the Jews?

7. What is the message of this chapter for you?

12

A Time to Remember

It would be an annual event from generation to generation, celebrated by every family . . . so that the memory of what had happened would never perish from the Jewish race (9:28, TLB).

Read Esther 9:19-32

Freed from the terror that must have hung over them like a pall, it was natural that the Jews would demonstrate their relief and release. So is it always when great deliverance comes to a people. Can you recall (if you are old enough) the great waves of jubilation when the glad news came at the end of World War II? People flocked into the streets. Perfect strangers hugged one another, and spontaneous singing broke out. My daughter pictured for me such scenes in the port city of Chittagong in December 1971 when the beleaguered people of Bangladesh learned of the enemy's surrender. The Bengalis danced in the street; even the normally burkah-veiled Muslim women threw back their veils and danced with the rest, for such emotions must have an out. And *Joi Bangla!* (victory to Bengal) was on the lips of young and old.

LEST WE FORGET

It must have been in the midst of such a scene that Mordecai, with the wisdom and foresight that has characterized him throughout, determined that this historic deliverance must never be allowed to be forgotten.

So another letter-writing project was initiated. (Some versions, notably the Apocrypha, speak of a book, rather than letters to record the happenings and immortalize them.)

This time the message is sent only to the *Jews* in the provinces of the Medo-Persian Empire.

There is no question about Mordecai's position of authority. The people receive his written instructions and undertake to heed them.

Mordecai reminds them of the sorrow that was turned into joy, the mourning into a good day. "Keep this date for a feast day, a day of joy when we send gifts to one another and remember to give especially to the poor," the letter instructs. It sounds like a Christmas letter.

There is not a word in it of all that Mordecai himself did in the situation. Haman is mentioned—the "enemy of the Jews"— and his plot that backfired. There is nothing to indicate that Mordecai had once been instrumental in saving the king's life—or of the fateful night when a sleepless king would have this event brought to his attention, with historic significance.

Esther is given full recognition for her resolve and bravery in coming before the king and all that came of her request for her people.

The story is recapped. A day is set aside to be perpetuated in Jewish history till this very day: the Feast of Purim. It became a two-day feast (9:17-21), from the evening that began the fourteenth day of the biblical month of Adar (February-March) through the fifteenth day.

On each of the feast days, the entire story of Esther is read in the synagogues, and three prayers are offered: a prayer of thanks that they are counted worthy to attend this service; a prayer of thanksgiving for the miraculous preservation of their ancestors; and praise that they have lived to observe another festival in memory of the deliverance.

One of the features of the Feast of Purim, even in this day, is that at each mention of Haman the congregation uses noisemakers to drown out the hated name.

WHY "PURIM"?

The name of the feast is interesting. From all the much more significant aspects of the whole dramatic plot and deliverance, they chose to highlight the fact that Haman had determined the day by lot "to find a lucky day for his venture" (3:7, Amplified). The Hebrew word for *lot* is *Pur,* and the plural *Purim.* A sidelight of this brings to mind that it is said of Adolph Hitler that he placed great faith in astrology. One day, so the story goes, an astrologer told Hitler he would die on a Jewish holiday. "Which one?" Hitler asked. The astrologer answered, *"Any* day you die would be a Jewish holiday."

Solemn indeed is the exhortation that Mordecai wrote, "That these days should be remembered and kept throughout every generation, every family, every province, and every city; and that these days of Purim should not fail from among the Jews, nor the memorial of them perish from their seed" (9:28).

There is a flavor of Gettysburg in these words: a vibrant loyalty that sees only right in calling to mind a day to remember in the history of a people.

What if as Christians, we were as diligent in keeping before our children the historic epics of our faith, with their deep, timeless, meaning!

THE VALUE OF REMEMBERING

Jewish holidays are much more meaningful to them than ours generally appear to be to us. They are part of their nationhood. We get together on the Fourth of July or, in Canada, on Dominion Day. Other nationalities and ethnic groups celebrate likewise (for example, the Irish on March 17). We may have a town parade, speeches, perhaps a fireworks display, but for the most part our national holidays are just that: holidays—picnics and parties and family get-togethers. When the Jewish people celebrate their holy days, however, the world community of Jews—the entire Jewish family—is getting together. And indubitably this has been largely instrumental in their retaining their distinctives as a people through their some thirty-five centuries. As *Christianity Today* points out in an editorial commemorating the state of Israel's twenty-fifth birthday,

> In purely human terms, Israel is rare indeed in having preserved a national continuity for so many centuries, during which time powerful empires and brilliant civilizations have risen and fallen. And it is unique in having survived almost twenty centuries of unbroken subjection to foreign powers and of dispersion among the other nations of the earth—the subjection dating from the occupation of Israel by Pompey the Great in 63 B.C. and the great dispersion from the conquest and destruction of rebellious Jerusalem by the Romans in A.D. 70. (The period of the Maccabees excepted, Israel had been under foreign control since Nebuchadnezzar.)[1]

The Jews can never get away from their remembrance of God. Some of them might be hard put to explain whether they remember God and therefore celebrate the holiday feasts, or celebrate the feasts, and this brings God to their remembrance. In the same manner, we might examine our Christian Easter and Christmas influx in our churches.

The Jewish feasts are rooted and grounded in God's special dealings with them.

How does the modern-day Jew celebrate Passover? I would be at the mercy of what I read and of what people tell me, except that it was my inestimable privilege some years ago to sit as a guest at the Passover feast in a Jewish home. These were not Hebrew Christians. They were not even particularly religious Jews. But this was Passover, and on that one night, *every* Jew is again in Egypt eating the lamb roast with fire, the unleavened bread, and the bitter herbs. An extra chair is placed for Elijah and the family participate in the age-old ritual. The son of the home asks, "What mean ye by this?" and the father repeats the story of the deliverance of the children of Israel

---

1. *Christianity Today,* 17 (May 11, 1973):27. Copyright 1973. Used by permission.

from their taskmasters. (See Exodus 12.) I sat entranced at that candlelit table.

So it is with the Jewish New Year and the Day of Atonement, these high holy days. I recall being mystified the first autumn we lived in New York. One September evening we found the usually hustle-bustle parkways deserted. We would walk up to a store in the area of Times Square, only to find it closed in the daytime. The term *Jewish holiday* is more than a kindly joke. It is a fact of Jewish life, for they take their Old Testament feast days seriously. These are their days to remember.

As long as there is a Feast of Purim, and there will be as long as the Jews congregate (see 9:27-28), there will be a remembering of Hitler as well as Haman.

Some say, "Why don't they forget Hitler and get on with Israel?" I personally heard and observed the reaction of some tourists, on a visit to Israel a few years ago. Atop Mt. Zion, near to the Tomb of David, were grisly mementoes of Buchenwald and Belsen. And people complained that these were on display. They might have been too young to remember the horrors—or had love of country and pride of race never been bred in them?

Patriotism is a healthy emotion. Love for one's country and people gives a sense of history and worth and a feeling of belonging. Born in Scotland, I can sit in St. Giles Cathedral in Edinburgh and fancy that I am breathing the same air that John Knox breathed in sixteenth century Scotland. I can empathize with my Jewish friends in their fervent nationalism. After all, they have more to boast of than the rest of us. *God* gave them their country. They are where they are by divine decree.

THE QUEEN WRITES A LETTER

We have not had the last of the letter writing in this ten-chapter book. This time Esther adds her personal confirmation.

In this instance, Esther's own ancestry is named: "Esther

the queen, the daugher of Abihail" (9:29), as though for once the record would have Mordecai appear in his own personal greatness and worth; not only as the kinsman of Queen Esther.

She wrote with authority—Esther, the *queen*, Esther, the Jewess.

No mention here or in the case of Mordecai's memorial letter, of sealing the letter with the king's ring. For no matter how cooperative or sympathetic to the cause of the Jews, no pagan king could dictate nor authorize a Jewish feast day.

What a contrast in the message of the letters that first were rushed post-haste into all the provinces: letters of doom. Now the posts go forth with their letters containing "words of peace and truth."

Is the analogy plain? Can there be either peace or truth while the enemy is allowed to cast dread over the nation? Can personal peace and truth bless us while we fail to break off diplomatic relations with the enemy of our soul who spells condemnation?

The decree of Esther confirmed these matters: the matters of a nation's Remembrance Day. Well might they remember Esther herself, the girl whose name means Star, for a star of hope rose for the nation when the Jewish Hadassah became the Medo-Persian Queen Esther.

And now wherever Jewish communities exist, however small, there is almost certain to be a Hadassah Society—and the 'Hadassah' is Esther of history. Jewish families—many non-Jewish likewise—name their daughters Esther.

In the great Hebrew University in Jerusalem, the medical center bears the name *Hadassah*.

The measure of Esther's and Mordecai's influence and importance is that this feast was indeed instituted. There seems to have been no "Thus saith the Lord, 'Thou shalt keep this day.' "

Some commentaries speak of the thirteenth day of the biblical month Adar as Esther's fast.[2]

2. *International Standard Bible Encyclopedia*, 2:1102.

To Think About and Do

1. Why is it important that memorial days be instituted and regularly observed to commemorate historic happenings? What are the benefits of such observance to a country and to individuals? What kind of loss results if there is no such time to remember?

2. What noble trait of Mordecai again comes to the fore in his letter?

3. If you were asked to explain the Feast of Purim, how would you do it? What would you emphasize?

4. What has the observance of their own holidays and feast days done, universally, for the Jewish people?

5. Take a few minutes to think over the significance of your own national holidays and evaluate what place and meaning they have in your personal and family life.

6. As Christians, what is our primary and ultimate citizenship? (see Ephesians 2:19-22). Discuss our bond as believers and our basis of hope for heavenly citizenship (John 14:1-6).

7. Why was the king's seal not used in the letters sent by Esther and Mordecai?

8. In what special way has Esther been immortalized by her people for her selfless heroism?

13

The Man the Bible Calls Great

He was, of course, very great among the Jews, and respected by all his countrymen . . . and was a friend at court for all of them (10:3, TLB).

Read Esther 10:1-3

People who achieve greatness, those whose names live on long after they have left earth's scene, rarely have gone in quest of immortality. They have done what came their way to do, and along the way it has become evident that they had come to the kingdom for a particular purpose. They have served their generation, and later generations still speak of them with admiration and reverence. Such was Mary with her alabaster box (Matthew 26:6-13). Such were Queen Esther and Mordecai.

CONFIRMING THE DATE

Ultimately they did recognize that what they had been privileged, under God, to do for their own people was worthy of a memorial. It was in the best interests of future generations that they not be allowed to forget. While Esther and Mordecai instituted the commemoration for this very purpose, it was the Jews of their own day who made this a personal responsibility.

The Jews ordained and took upon them, and upon their seed, and upon all such as joined themselves unto them, so as

101

it should not fail, that they would keep these two days according to their . . . appointed time every year; and that these days
should be remembered and kept throughout every generation, every family, every province, and every city; and that
these days of Purim should not fail from among the Jews,
nor the memorial of them perish from their seed (9:27-28).

No provision made here for juggling the day and the date to
allow for a three-day weekend. What are we giving up in
meaningfulness when we accommodate our national historic
dates to our own desires for a prolonged holiday? Are we
robbing our children of some of their heritage as they see the
emphasis as much (sometimes more) on fun and enjoyment,
than on commemorating a highlight of our nationhood or of
our heroes?

Well might the Jews remember Esther! But, no less was this
an event for every Christian to be thankful, because Esther's
selflessness, in the providence of God, kept alive the line
through whom our Saviour came.

SOMETHING TO REMEMBER YOU BY

It may never be given us in our lifetime to know why we
"came to the kingdom." Yet there is in every person that
yearning to do something—even one thing—that will be remembered when we are gone.

I recall one time receiving a phone call in my office at the
Narramore Christian Foundation. The caller was a distraught
woman who had unadvisedly contracted with a company to
publish a book she had written. She had apparently not understood all of her own responsibility in such an undertaking, and
she now found herself saddled with a stack of books for sale,
and owing more money than she could possibly pay the pub-
lisher. I listened as she poured out this tale, and I admit that
I became very angry at "the party of the second part."

Later that day, I ventilated my feelings of outrage to Dr.
Narramore. I was not very kind—not even objective— in my
denunciation of "such a publishing company." I recall that

he listened, then he said something to the effect that such companies do serve a purpose, for there are people who will give everything they possess in this world to assure that something lives on beyond their own life span.

Esther had not deliberately striven to do this, but her selflessness and spirit of willing sacrifice won her a place in history.

We are not Esther. We are not Mordecai, but surely we can do something that will count in time—and beyond ourselves. It may be in the principles we daily inculcate in our own children; standards and values that will live on even in their children. Then, too, we can be instrumental, under God, in leading someone to Christ. There is something that will live on! And *you* can do it.

One of my own Sunday school teachers related this to me. She had for some years taught a class of girls in their late teens and into their twenties. The class had wanted to keep her for their teacher, and she had become a real counselor and a friend to them. But one Sunday afternoon her own young daughter saw her mother sitting by the fireplace with a troubled look on her usually serene face.

"What's wrong, Mama?" her daughter asked. "You look so sad."

"Oh, it's my class, dear. I think I'll give up teaching. I don't seem to be getting anywhere with my girls. It seems the Lord's not using me anymore."

The mother would have continued, but her daughter cut in, "Mama, don't *ever* say that! *You led me to the Lord.*"

I have known of this girl through the years since. Although her mother has gone into the presence of the Saviour she loved and served, this daughter is still a tribute to her mother's faithfulness. This Sunday school teacher and mother left something that lives on and will live on.

Generally, I have observed, God uses us in the area of our own greatest interests to be an influence on others. Ours has always been a missions-conscious family. One Sunday just after we had moved to a new church, I was in the choir room when the first choir member came to don her robe for the evening service. We were alone for a few minutes, and as I engaged her in conversation, I learned that she was a highly trained laboratory technician and that she also had graduated from a Christian college.

"Have you ever thought," "I asked her, "that a trained technician such as yourself can almost double the effectiveness of a doctor on the mission field? Have you ever thought of being a foreign missionary?"

We talked a little more. But apparently that first seed dropped on good ground. For more than ten years this girl has served in the Philippines, and never a month has passed but that she has written me a letter telling of her opportunities in the medical and evangelistic areas, and of some triumphs along the way.

Esther did not write a book that would immortalize her— but another, inspired by God, did.

God is writing a book, the Bible tells us (Malachi 3:16-17)—a book of remembrance. And we can get our names in that, just for thinking about Him and talking to each other about Him. (Apart from the immortal dividends of this constant sense of "God with us," we also enjoy the present good effects. When we are dwelling on God and His goodness to us, Satan has a hard time trying to discourage us.)

THE MAN THE BIBLE CALLS GREAT

The drama closes, not with the heroine queen, but with her foster father, Mordecai. Position, wealth, the royal robes, a crown—none of these or all of them together had changed this man. He leaves the scene the same admirable character we first met: Mordecai the Jew, loyal to his people and religion, loyal to the king, humble, self-effacing, but amply able and willing to take action when this is called for. His acts, his power, his might, and his greatness are not only commemorated by his own people. They are written in the chronicles of the kings of Media and Persia. So it is that sometimes in the course of doing God's will—doing our work for God well and with dedication—even the secular world takes notice and includes it in their records. So we have among the greats immortalized in Westminster Abbey a Livingstone, a humble Scottish missionary who made his contribution to Africa and the world, in the course of doing God's will for his life. And he is but one. God still has his great men and women (the greatest not being aware that they are great). We can take heart, then, and keep in mind the verse, "Let us not be weary in well-doing: for in due season we shall reap, if we faint not" (Galatians 6:9).

God is taking notice of where we are, of what we are doing, and how we are doing it for Him. "For God is not unrighteous to forget your work and labour of love, which ye have showed in His name" (Hebrews 6:10).

To each of us come opportunities to be great for God.

In this man Mordecai we find a rare combination: the ability to rise to fantastic heights of personal importance and still retain the favor of his own people, approximating in this, our Lord who "increased in wisdom . . . and in favour with God and man" (Luke 2:52).

The secret of Mordecai's popularity with the people is not hard to find. His concern, far from furthering his own interests, was in "seeking the wealth of his people, and speaking peace to all his seed" (10:3).

Privilege brings responsibility. As was true of Esther, so it applies to Mordecai. It is a mark of his greatness that this man who had imposed this type of responsible thinking upon a young woman in a place of privilege carries it out in his own life.

There are times and occasions when, because of one's position of privilege, we must put the welfare of other people before our personal comfort, pleasure, and even safety.

Mordecai served his generation. He too "came to the kingdom for such a time."

Have you ever pondered how many such biblical expressions become a part of our language? I think of such sayings as "the handwriting on the wall," "weighed in the balances," "the wisdom of Solomon," "out of the mouths of babes," and, as the prototype of ideal friendship, "David and Jonathan," to mention just a few. They appear in literature as well as in everyday conversation and it is easily apparent when a person knows the Bible and when he does not. This is one more brief for being a Bible scholar and for inculcating in our children a love for the Scriptures and a sense of their worth. Without such knowledge we have no frame of reference for hundreds of references and inferences that have their source in the Bible. The works of Shakespeare, for example, abound in biblical sayings and allusions. Some of the most famous and historic speeches include verses from the Holy Scriptures.

THE KING ON GOD'S CHESS BOARD

Did the great Emperor Ahasuerus ever realize that he too came to the kingdom for such a time as this or that his choice of a queen to replace the disobedient Vashti was in the hands of the Lord God of the Jews? Did he many times ponder the sleepless night and all that came of it?

And would he ever come to the realization that the God of the Jews holds the whole world in His hands?

Secular history points to the fact that the events recorded in the book of Esther had even longer-range effects than the victory of the thirteenth of Adar. The favored queen was still a powerful figure some thirty years later when Nehemiah needed a friend at court. The fact that the queen was a Jewess must have been reflected in the attitude of everyone toward the Jews. Undoubtedly the Jews' stock had risen as the man, Mordecai the Jew, rose ever higher in rank, in the esteem likewise of his people, and in the sight of the king on his throne. Thus a favorable climate was being established for the day when Nehemiah would make his historic plea for the rebuilding of the ruined walls of Jerusalem; when he would pray to the God of heaven, and then speak to the king (see Neh 2:4-6). This king, Artaxerxes, (Neh 1:11) was a stepson of Queen Esther. That fact must have given the Jews great prestige at the Persian court. *Halley's Bible Handbook* states, "Esther was most probably still alive, and an influential personage in the palace, when both Ezra and Nehemiah went to Jerusalem. Our guess is that we have Esther to thank for Artaxerxes' kindly feeling toward the Jews, and his interest in having Jerusalem rebuilt."[1]

The book of Esther may seem to drop off the end with the three-verse chapter 10.

It may, then, be of interest to you to read the expanded account as recorded in the Apocrypha (now included in the New English Bible). Interestingly, there is no lack of mention of the name of God. For example, in writing of Haman's dastardly plot, Artaxerxes the king states,

> The Jews whom the triple-dyed villain had consigned to extinction, are no evil-doers . . . they are the children of the Living God, most high, most mighty, who maintains the empire in most wonderful order, for us as for our ancestors . . . disregard the letters of Haman because God who is Lord of all having speedily brought upon him the punishment that he deserved (Rest of Esther 16:15-18 [Apocrypha], NEB).

THE LESSON OF THE BOOK

Looking for a key word in this book of the Bible that somehow never once names the name of God, we are convinced this word must be *providence*. An overshadowing providence governs with an unseen hand.

The book of Esther would teach us:

1. God knows what is going on in the affairs of man and his world.
2. God has a settled, long-range plan—not a five-year, or a ten-year scheme dependent on how things mature.

1. *Halley's Bible Handbook,* 24th ed. (Grand Rapids: Zondervan), pp. 235. 237.

3. God's plan is carried out by individuals for whom He has a plan. God chooses and uses certain men and women—the real stars in His drama of history—men and women whom He can trust to rise to the challenge of a crucial time, even though this means determining "If I perish, I perish!"
4. God uses others—men in high places who all unknowingly many times, are nevertheless carrying forward God's master plan for those who are His people.
5. God's alarm clock strikes exactly at the right moment.

The book of Esther would teach even the most casual reader the ultimate triumph of right over wrong. We can take heart then, in our own age with its unprecedented confusion and misery, knowing that God is still on His throne And He *will* remember His own (Psalm 11:4).

He will bring to the kingdom the right man, the right woman for such a time as this—even if He has to keep a king awake all night in order to accomplish His purpose!

To Think About and Do

1. Ultimately, what did the survival of the Jewish people mean to the rest of the world?
2. What thoughts do you have concerning your doing something that will outlast you? What do you dream of doing? What might you possibly do? What are some of the things everyone can do that might have lasting effect?
3. In what particular areas of influence will you be accountable to God?
4. If you sometimes become discouraged in your service for the Lord, what Scripture verses should inspire and encourage you?
5. How do you personally react to the statement "to each of us come opportunities to be great for God"? Are you challenged by it, or do you consider it to mean "everybody but me"?

6. What made Mordecai popular with his own people? (Frequently people resent it when one of their own rises to great heights.)

7. Since, obviously, many quotations from the Bible are in common use, what does it denote when a person does not understand their implication? It would be an interesting exercise listing as many as you can find.

8. What is your thinking concerning Ahasuerus' place in God's plan?

9. What long-term influence did Esther wield in her lifetime?

10. Reread the entire book of Esther, especially noting the "if" situations: for example, "if Mordecai had not overheard the assassination plot;" "if the king had been sleepless just one night later."

11. Enumerate and, if in a group, discuss in depth the practical lessons which this ten-chapter book of the Old Testament teaches us for our own day.